YR EGLWYS THE CHURCH
YNG NGHYMRU IN WALES

LECTIONARY

Year C

Weekdays 1

Advent
2024

~

Kingdom
2025

Compiled by
Ritchie Craven

Contents	page
Lectionary explanation and use	2
BOOK ONE: Detailed Lectionary	5
Alternative readings	112
Replaced readings	115
Days of Special Prayers	120
BOOK TWO: Holy Days and other services	121
Rogation and Ember Days	154
Thanksgiving Festivals	155
Dedication Festival	156
Eucharistic Commons	157

NEW ...

... 'Daily with God' is designed to offer you the opportunity to shape a pattern of prayer which suits you. It includes some of the greatest and best-loved prayers of Christians down through the ages. It gives you a core of prayers to use daily as you approach the throne of God's grace, together with prayers for particular occasions and opportunities.

£12.99
including UK postage and packing (Bilingual).

Available from Y Lolfa:
www.ylolfa.com

Year

Within the Lectionary, all celebrations are shown on their correct day including those falling on a Sunday. Holy Days and Festivals in groups I and II should always be celebrated and those in group II which are displaced are normally celebrated on the next available day (but may be celebrated on any convenient day before the next Sunday).

If St David falls on Ash Wednesday it is transferred to the previous day.

Lesser Festivals and Commemorations in groups IV and V are optional and are not normally transferred.

The provision is given for all celebrations at the back section of the book (starting on page 121).

Note

On those occasions when a Holy Day or Festival from groups I or II replaces a Sunday in Ordinary Time, the readings appointed for the Eucharist are the Principal Service readings, those appointed for Evening Prayer are the Second Service readings and those appointed for Morning Prayer are the Third Service Readings.

Groups I, II and III: The Eucharist and Daily Offices are of the day, normally with lectionary provision. Daily Eucharistic provision is omitted and Daily Office material may be combined on the preceding and/or following weekday. The collect used is that of the day.

Groups IV and V: The Daily Offices are of the ordinary day or season, and the collect is normally that of the week although the collect of the day may be used, especially if there is not a celebration of the Eucharist that day. At weekday celebrations of Lesser Festivals in group IV the Daily Eucharist readings are normally used but may be replaced by proper readings. At weekday celebrations of Commemorations in group V the Daily Eucharist readings are normally used.

A Patronal Festival, Feast of Title, Dedication Festival or Provincial, Diocesan, Ecumenical celebration or Harvest Thanksgiving (traditionally around the first Sunday of October) may take precedence of any Sunday or other observance in groups III - V.

Octaves are observed at the feasts of Christmas and Easter only. Easter-tide begins on Easter Eve and ends on the Day of Pentecost.

Psalms: The references to psalms in the lectionary refer to the verses as they appear in scripture rather than in any liturgical form of the Psalter.

Morning and Evening Prayer during Holy Week

The readings for Mattins and Evensong are taken from the second and third provision as appropriate.

The Collect

It should be normal to use one collect of the day, as appropriate to the lections in use. The Post Communion prayer is optional and matches the collect.

Colours

The colour scheme listed in the Lectionary is that agreed by the Bench of Bishops in June 2011 and reflects the most widespread current practise.

For major saints' day and special services e.g. confirmations, inductions, funerals etc. other appropriate colours may be worn.

Sundays and Seasons - Advent in PURPLE; Christmas Day to Candlemas (2nd February) in WHITE; 3rd February to Shrove Tuesday in GREEN; Ash Wednesday until eve of Palm Sunday in PURPLE (although PASSION RED may be worn for Passion Sunday, PASSION RED is a dark mulberry red as distinct from the more Pentecostal red); Palm Sunday and Holy Week in PASSION RED or PURPLE, except the Eucharist on Maundy Thursday in WHITE. Lenten array may be worn during Lent or just in Holy Week; Easter Day to the eve of Pentecost in WHITE;

Pentecost Sunday in RED and the Monday after Pentecost to eve of Advent Sunday in GREEN with the exception of Trinity Sunday in WHITE. (RED as option for Kingdom Season). Christ the King in WHITE.

Holy Days

Feasts of the Blessed Virgin Mary, Joseph of Nazareth, Birth of John the Baptist, Mary Magdalene, Transfiguration, Michael and All Angels, John the Evangelist, Thanksgiving for the Holy Communion in WHITE;

Apostles and Evangelists (except John the Evangelist), Holy Cross Day, Holy Innocents in RED;

All Souls' Day in PURPLE (or Black);

Lesser Festivals (IV) in RED (for Martyrs) or WHITE or the colour of the season;

Commemorations (V) normally in the colour of the season but RED (for Martyrs) or WHITE may be used if desired.

DETAILED LECTIONARY

BOOK ONE:

Year C

Weekdays 1

Advent
2024

~

Kingdom
2025

THE FIRST SUNDAY of ADVENT

DATE	COLLECT & PC	PRINCIPAL SERVICE
Sunday 1 December (†) World AIDS Day	1 & 2	Jeremiah 33. 14-16 Psalm 25. 1-10 1 Thessalonians 3. 9-13 Luke 21. 25-36

† The Saints, Martyrs and Missionaries *of* Asia	† Francis Xavier	
Monday 2 December	Tuesday 3 December	Wednesday 4 December
DAILY EUCHARIST		
Collect & PC 1 & 2 Isaiah 4. 2-6 Psalm 122 Matthew 8. 5-13	Collect & PC 1 & 2 Isaiah 11. 1-10 Psalm 72. 1-8 Luke 10. 21-24	Collect & PC 1 & 2 Isaiah 25. 6-9 Psalm 23 Matthew 15. 29-39
Morning Prayer		
Psalm 50; [54] Isaiah 42. 18-end Revelation 19	Psalm 80; [82] Isaiah 43. 1-13 Revelation 20	Psalm [5;] 7 Isaiah 43. 14-end Revelation 21. 1-8
Evening Prayer		
Psalm [70;] 71 Isaiah 25. 1-9 Matthew 12. 1-21	Psalm 74; [75] Isaiah 26. 1-13 Matthew 12. 22-37	Psalm [76;] 77 Isaiah 28. 1-13 Matthew 12. 38-end

Advent 2024 - Kingdom 2025

THIRD SERVICE	SECOND SERVICE	Notes
Psalm 44 Isaiah 51. 4-11 Romans 13. 11-14	Psalm 9 *or* 9. 1-8 Joel 3. 9-21 Revelation 14.13 – 15.4 *If the Second Service is a Eucharist, the Gospel is:* John 3. 1-17	1984 BCP page 27. † For weekday commemorations see page 122 & 123.

	† Nicholas	† Ambrose
Thursday 5 December	**Friday 6 December**	**Saturday 7 December**
DAILY EUCHARIST		
Collect & PC 1 & 2 Isaiah 26. 1-6 Psalm 118. 19-24 Matthew 7. 21-27	Collect & PC 1 & 2 Isaiah 29. 17-24 Psalm 27. 1-4, 13, 14 Matthew 9. 27-31	Collect & PC 1 & 2 Isaiah 30. 19-21, 23-26 Psalm 147. 1-11 Matthew 9.35 – 10.1, 5-8
	Morning Prayer	
Psalm 42; [43] Isaiah 44. 1-8 Revelation 21. 9-21	Psalm 25; [26] Isaiah 44. 9-23 Revelation 21.22 – 22.5	Psalm 9 Isaiah 44.24 – 45.13 Revelation 22. 6-end
	Evening Prayer	
Psalm 40; [46] Isaiah 28. 14-end Matthew 13. 1-23	Psalm [16;] 17 Isaiah 29. 1-14 Matthew 13. 24-43	Psalm 27; 28 Isaiah 29. 15-end Matthew 13. 44-end

THE SECOND SUNDAY of ADVENT

DATE	COLLECT & PC	PRINCIPAL SERVICE
Sunday 8 December (†)	3 & 4	Baruch 5. 1-9 *or* Malachi 3. 1-4 *Canticle*: Benedictus (Luke 1. 68-79) Philippians 1. 3-11 Luke 3. 1-6

Monday 9 December	Tuesday 10 December	Ember Day Wednesday 11 December
DAILY EUCHARIST		
Collect & PC 3 & 4 Isaiah 35. 1-10 Psalm 85. 8-13 Luke 5. 17-26	Collect & PC 3 & 4 Isaiah 40. 1-11 Psalm 96 Matthew 18. 12-14	Collect & PC 351 & 352 Ember set 1, 2 *or* 3. See page 154.
Morning Prayer		
Psalm 44 Isaiah 45. 14-end 1 Thessalonians 1	Psalm 56; [57] Isaiah 46 1 Thessalonians 2. 1-12	Psalm 62; [63] Isaiah 47 1 Thessalonians 2. 13-end
Evening Prayer		
Psalm 144, [146] Isaiah 30. 1-18 Matthew 14. 1-12	Psalm 11; [12; 13] Isaiah 30. 19-end Matthew 14. 13-end	Psalm 10; [14] Isaiah 31 Matthew 15. 1-20

Advent 2024 - Kingdom 2025

THIRD SERVICE	SECOND SERVICE	Notes
Psalm 80 Isaiah 64. 1-7 Matthew 11. 2-11	Psalm 75; [76] Isaiah 40. 1-11 Luke 1. 1-25	1984 BCP page 30. † For weekday commemorations see page 123.

	† Lucy	† John of the Cross
	Ember Day	Ember Day
Thursday 12 December	Friday 13 December	Saturday 14 December
DAILY EUCHARIST		
Collect & PC 3 & 4 Isaiah 41. 13-20 Psalm 145. 1-4, 8-13 Matthew 11. 7-15	Collect & PC 351 & 352 Ember set 1, 2 *or* 3. See page 154.	Collect & PC 351 & 352 Ember set 1, 2 *or* 3. See page 154.
Morning Prayer		
Psalm [53;] 54; [60] Isaiah 48. 1-11 1 Thessalonians 3	Psalm [85;] 86 Isaiah 48. 12-end 1 Thessalonians 4. 1-12	Psalm 145 Isaiah 49. 1-13 1 Thessalonians 4. 13-end
Evening Prayer		
Psalm 73 Isaiah 32 Matthew 15. 21-28	Psalm [82;] 90 Isaiah 33. 1-22 Matthew 15. 29-end	Psalm [93;] 94 Isaiah 35 Matthew 16. 1-12

THE THIRD SUNDAY *of* ADVENT

DATE	COLLECT & PC	PRINCIPAL SERVICE
Sunday 15 December	5 & 6	Zephaniah 3. 14-20 *Canticle*: Isaiah 12. 2-6; *or* Psalm 146. 5-10 Philippians 4. 4-7 Luke 3. 7-18

Monday 16 December	O Wisdom! Tuesday 17 December	O Adonai! Wednesday 18 December
DAILY EUCHARIST		
Collect & PC 5 & 6 Numbers 24. 2-7, 15-17a Psalm 25. 4-10 Matthew 21. 23-27	Collect & PC 324 & 6 Genesis 49. 2, 8-10 Psalm 72. 1-8 Matthew 1. 1-7, 17	Collect & PC 325 & 6 Jeremiah 23. 5-8 Psalm 72. 11-20 Matthew 1. 18-25
Morning Prayer		
Psalm 40 Isaiah 49. 14-25 1 Thessalonians 5. 1-11	Psalm 70; [74] Isaiah 50 1 Thessalonians 5. 12-end	Psalm 75; [96] Isaiah 51. 1-8 2 Thessalonians 1
Evening Prayer		
Psalm [25;] 26 Isaiah 38. 1-8, 21-22 Matthew 16. 13-end	Psalm 50; [54] Isaiah 38. 9-20 Matthew 17. 1-13	Psalm [25;] 82 Isaiah 39 Matthew 17. 14-21

Advent 2024 - Kingdom 2025

THIRD SERVICE	SECOND SERVICE	Notes
Psalm 12; 14 Isaiah 25. 1-9 1 Corinthians 4. 1-5	Psalm 50. 1-6; [62] Isaiah 35 Luke 1. 57-66, [67-80]	1984 BCP page 33.

O Root of Jesse! Thursday 19 December	O Key of David! Friday 20 December	O Dayspring! Saturday 21 December
DAILY EUCHARIST		
Collect & PC 326 & 6 Judges 13. 2-7, 24, 25 Psalm 71. 1-8 Luke 1. 5-25	Collect & PC 327 & 6 Isaiah 7. 10-14 Psalm 24 Luke 1. 26-38	Collect & PC 328 & 6 Zephaniah 3. 14-18 Psalm 33. 1-5, 18-22 Luke 1. 39-45
Morning Prayer		
Psalm [144,] 146 Zephaniah 1.1 – 2.3 2 Thessalonians 2	Psalm 46; [95] Isaiah 51. 17-end 2 Thessalonians 3	Psalm 121; [122; 123] Isaiah 52. 1-12 Jude
Evening Prayer		
Psalm [10;] 57 Isaiah 51. 9-16 Matthew 17. 22-end	Psalm 4; [9] Zephaniah 3. 1-13 Matthew 18. 1-20	Psalm [80;] 84 Zephaniah 3. 14-end Matthew 18. 21-end

Year C - Weekdays 1

THE FOURTH SUNDAY of ADVENT

DATE	COLLECT & PC	PRINCIPAL SERVICE
Sunday 22 December	7 & 8	Micah 5. 2-5a *Canticle:* Magnificat (Luke 1. 47-55) *or* Psalm 80. 1-7 Hebrews 10. 5-10 Luke 1. 39-45, [46-55]

O Emmanuel! Monday 23 December	Christmas Eve* Tuesday 24 December	THE NATIVITY OF OUR LORD Christmas Day Wednesday 25 December
DAILY EUCHARIST		**PRINCIPAL SERVICE**
Collect & PC 330 & 8 Malachi 3. 1-5 Psalm 25. 1-15 Luke 1. 57-66	Collect & PC 9 & 10 *Eucharist during the Day:* 2 Samuel 7. 1-5, 8-11, 16 Psalm 89. 2, 21-27 Acts 13. 16-26 Luke 1. 67-79	Collect & PC 11 & 12 *Any of the following sets of readings at the bottom of page 13* may be used on the evening of Christmas Eve and on Christmas Day.* *Set III should be used at some service during the celebration.*
Morning Prayer		**THIRD SERVICE**
Psalm [128; 129;] 130; [131] Isaiah 52.13 – *end of* 53 2 Peter 1. 1-15	Psalm 45; [113] Isaiah 54 2 Peter 1.16 – 2.3	Psalm 110 Isaiah 62. 1-5 Matthew 1. 18-25
Evening Prayer		**SECOND SERVICE**
Psalm 89. 1-37 Malachi 1. 1, 6-end Matthew 19. 1-12	Psalm 85 Zechariah 2 Revelation 1. 1-8	Psalm 8 Isaiah 65. 17-25 Philippians 2. 5-11 *or* Luke 2. 1-20 *if it has not be used at the Principal Service of the day.*

Advent 2024 - Kingdom 2025

THIRD SERVICE	SECOND SERVICE	Notes
Psalm 144 Isaiah 32. 1-8 Revelation 22. 6-21	Psalm 123; [131] Isaiah 10.33 – 11.10 Matthew 1. 18-25	1984 BCP page 35.
		Day of Prayer for Refugees

Stephen, Deacon and First Martyr **Thursday 26 December**	John, Apostle and Evangelist Friday 27 December	The Innocents **Saturday 28 December**
DAILY EUCHARIST		
Collect & PC 331 & 12 2 Chronicles 24. 20-22 Psalm 119. 161-168 Acts 7. 51-60 Matthew 23. 34-39 *or* Acts 7. 51-60 Psalm 119. 161-168 Galatians 2. 16b-20 Matthew 23. 34-39	Collect & PC 332 & 12 (Day) Exodus 33. 7-11a Psalm 117 1 John 1 John 21. 19b-25	Collect & PC 333 & 385 / 389 Jeremiah 31. 15-17 Psalm 124 1 Corinthians 1. 26-29 Matthew 2. 13b-18
Morning Prayer		
Psalm 13; [31. 1-8; 150] Jeremiah 26. 12-15 Acts 6	Psalm 21; [147. 13-end] Exodus 33. 7-11a 1 John 2. 1-11	Psalm 36; [146] Baruch 4. 21-27 *or* Genesis 37. 13-20 Matthew 18. 1-10
Evening Prayer		
Psalm [57;] 86 Genesis 4. 1-10 Matthew 10. 17-22	Psalm 97 Isaiah 6. 1-8, [9, 10] 1 John 5. 1-12	Psalm [123;] 128 Isaiah 49. 14-25 Mark 10. 13-16
Set I Isaiah 9. 2-7 Psalm 96 Titus 2. 11-14 Luke 2. 1-14, [15-20]	*Set II* Isaiah 62. 6-12 Psalm 97 Titus 3. 4-7 Luke 2. [1-7,] 8-20	*Set III* Isaiah 52. 7-10 Psalm 98 Hebrews 1. 1-4, [5-12] John 1. 1-14

*→ ⁎

Year C - Weekdays 1

THE FIRST SUNDAY of CHRISTMAS

DATE	COLLECT & PC	PRINCIPAL SERVICE
Sunday 29 December (†)	13 & 14	1 Samuel 2. 18-20, 26 Psalm 148 *or* 148. 7-14 Colossians 3. 12-17 Luke 2. 41-52

		2025
† Tathan	† John Wycliffe	The Naming of Jesus
Monday 30 December	Tuesday 31 December	Wednesday 1 January
DAILY EUCHARIST		
Collect & PC 13 & 14 1 John 2. 12-17 Psalm 96. 7-10 Luke 2. 36-40	Collect & PC 13 & 14 1 John 2. 18-21 Psalm 96. 1, 2, 11-13 John 1. 1-18	Collect & PC 142 & 14 Numbers 6. 22-27 Psalm 8 Galatians 4. 4-7 Luke 2. 15-21
Morning Prayer		
Psalm [111; 112;] 113 Isaiah 59. 1-15a John 1. 19-28	Psalm 102 Isaiah 59. 15b-end John 1. 29-34	Psalm 103; [150] Genesis 17. 1-13 Romans 2. 17-29
Evening Prayer		
Psalm 65; [84] Jonah 2 Colossians 1. 15-23	Psalm 90; [148] Jonah 3 – 4 Colossians 1.24 – 2.7	Psalm 115 Deuteronomy 30. (1-10,) 11-20 Acts 3. 1-16

... on the eve of the Naming of Jesus:
Psalm 148: Jeremiah 23. 1-6: Colossians 2. 8-15

Advent 2024 - Kingdom 2025

THIRD SERVICE	SECOND SERVICE	Notes
Psalm 105. 1-11 Isaiah 41.21 – 42.1 1 John 1. 1-7	Psalm 132 Isaiah 61 Galatians 3.27 – 4.7 *If the Second Service is a Eucharist, the Gospel is:* Luke 2. 15-21	1984 BCP page 43. † For weekday commemorations see page 124.

	† Morris Williams	
Thursday 2 January	Friday 3 January	Saturday 4 January
DAILY EUCHARIST		
Collect & PC 13 & 14 1 John 2. 22-29 Psalm 98. 1-4 John 1. 19-28	Collect & PC 13 & 14 1 John 3. 1-6 Psalm 98. 1-6 John 1. 29-34	Collect & PC 13 & 14 1 John 3. 7-10 Psalm 98. 1, 2, 7-9 John 1. 35-42
Morning Prayer		
Psalm 18. 1-30 Isaiah 60. 1-12 John 1. 35-42	Psalm 127; [128; 131] Isaiah 60. 13-end John 1. 43-end	Psalm 89. 1-37 Isaiah 61 John 2. 1-12
Evening Prayer		
Psalm [45;] 46 Ruth 1 Colossians 2. 8-end	Psalm 2; [110] Ruth 2 Colossians 3. 1-11	Psalm [85;] 87 Ruth 3 Colossians 3.12 – 4.1

Year C - Weekdays 1

* THE SECOND SUNDAY *of* CHRISTMAS

DATE	COLLECT & PC	PRINCIPAL SERVICE	
Sunday 5 January	15 & 16	*Either:* Jeremiah 31. 7-14 Psalm 147. 12-20 Ephesians 1. 3-14 John 1. [1-9,] 10-18	*or:* Sirach 24. 1-12 *Canticle:* Wisdom 10. 15-21 Ephesians 1. 3-14 John 1. [1-9,] 10-18

* In this sequence, the Epiphany of Our Lord can be moved to this Sunday. Readings for Monday 6 January can be found on page 112.

* THE EPIPHANY OF OUR LORD Monday 6 January	Tuesday 7 January	Wednesday 8 January
PRINCIPAL SERVICE	**DAILY EUCHARIST**	
Collect & PC 17 & 18 Isaiah 60. 1-6 Psalm 72. [1-9,] 10-15 Ephesians 3. 1-12 Matthew 2. 1-12	Collect & PC 15 & 16 1 John 3.19 – 4.6 Psalm 2 Matthew 4. 12-17, 23-25	Collect & PC 15 & 16 1 John 4. 7-12 Psalm 72. 1-8 Mark 6. 30-44
THIRD SERVICE	**Morning Prayer**	
Psalm 113; 132 Jeremiah 31. 7-14 John 1. 29-34	Psalm 99; [147. 1-12] Isaiah 63. 7-end 1 John 3	Psalm 46; [147. 13-end] Isaiah 64 1 John 4. 7-end
SECOND SERVICE	**Evening Prayer**	
Psalm 98; 100 Baruch 4.36 – 5.9 *or* Isaiah 60. 1-9 John 2. 1-11	Psalm 118 Baruch 1. 15 – 2.10 *or* Jeremiah 23. 1-8 Matthew 20. 1-16	Psalm 145 Baruch 2. 11-end *or* Jeremiah 30. 1-17 Matthew 20. 17-28

Advent 2024 - Kingdom 2025

THIRD SERVICE	SECOND SERVICE	Notes
Psalm 87 Isaiah 12 2 Thessalonians 2. 1-8	Psalm 135 1 Samuel 1. 20-28 1 John 4. 7-16 *If the Second Service is a Eucharist, the Gospel is:* **Matthew 2. 13-23**	1984 BCP page 45. † For weekday commemorations see page 125.

On the eve of the Epiphany: Psalm 96; 97: Isaiah 49. 1-13: John 4. 7-26

	† William Laud	† Rhys Prichard; William Williams and Isaac Williams
Thursday 9 January	Friday 10 January	Saturday 11 January

DAILY EUCHARIST

Collect & PC 15 & 16 1 John 4. 11-19 Psalm 72. 1,2, 10-13 Mark 6. 45-52	Collect & PC 15 & 16 1 John 4.19 – 5.4 Psalm 72. 1,2, 14-20 Luke 4. 14-22	Collect & PC 15 & 16 1 John 5. 5-12 Psalm 147. 12-20 Luke 5. 12-16

Morning Prayer

Psalm [2;] 148 Isaiah 65. 1-16 1 John 5. 1- 12	Psalm [97;] 149 Isaiah 65. 17-end 1 John 5. 13-end	Psalm [98;] 150 Isaiah 66. 1-11 2 John

Evening Prayer

Psalm 67; [72] Baruch 3. 1-8 *or* Jeremiah 30.18 – 31.9 Matthew 20. 29-end	Psalm [27;] 29 Baruch 3.9 – 4.4 *or* Jeremiah 31. 10-17 Matthew 23. 1-12	Psalm 93; [132] Baruch 4. 21-30 *or* Jeremiah 33. 14-end Matthew 23. 13-28

... on the eve of the Baptism of Christ:
Psalm 36: Isaiah 61: Titus 2. 11-14; 3. 4-7

THE BAPTISM OF CHRIST - THE FIRST SUNDAY of EPIPHANY

DATE	COLLECT & PC	PRINCIPAL SERVICE
Sunday 12 January	19 & 20	Isaiah 43. 1-7 Psalm 29 Acts 8. 14-17 Luke 3. 15-17, 21-22

† Hilary	† Kentigern	
Monday 13 January	Tuesday 14 January	Wednesday 15 January
DAILY EUCHARIST		
Collect & PC 19 & 20 Hebrews 1. 1-6 Psalm 97. 1-2, 6-10 Mark 1. 14-20	Collect & PC 19 & 20 Hebrews 2. 5-12 Psalm 8 Mark 1. 21-28	Collect & PC 19 & 20 Hebrews 2. 14-end Psalm 105. 1-9 Mark 1. 29-39
Morning Prayer		
Psalm 2; [110] Amos 1 1 Corinthians 1. 1-17	Psalm [8;] 9 Amos 2 1 Corinthians 1. 18-end	Psalm [19;] 20 Amos 3 1 Corinthians 2
Evening Prayer		
Psalm 34; [36] Genesis 1. 1-19 Matthew 21. 1-17	Psalm 45; [46] Genesis 1.20 – 2.3 Matthew 21. 18-32	Psalm 47; [48] Genesis 2. 4-end Matthew 21. 33-end

Advent 2024 - Kingdom 2025

THIRD SERVICE	SECOND SERVICE	Notes
Psalm 89. 19-29 Isaiah 42. 1-9 Acts 19. 1-7	Psalm 46; 47 Isaiah 55. 1-11 Romans 6. 1-11 *If the Second Service is a Eucharist, the Gospel is:* **Mark 1. 4-11**	1984 BCP page 50. † For weekday commemorations see page 125 & 126.

	† Antony *of* Egypt	18-25 January: Week of Prayers for Christian Unity. † The Confession of Peter
Thursday 16 January	Friday 17 January	Saturday 18 January
DAILY EUCHARIST		
Collect & PC 19 & 20 Hebrews 3. 7-14 Psalm 95. 1, 8-end Mark 1. 40-end	Collect & PC 19 & 20 Hebrews 4. 1-4, 11 Psalm 78. 3-8 Mark 2. 1-12	Collect & PC 19 & 20 Hebrews 4. 12-end Psalm 19. 7-end Mark 2. 13-17
Morning Prayer		
Psalm 21; [24] Amos 4 1 Corinthians 3	Psalm 67; [72] Amos 5. 1-17 1 Corinthians 4	Psalm [29;] 33 Amos 5. 18-end 1 Corinthians 5
Evening Prayer		
Psalm 61; [65] Genesis 3 Matthew 22. 1-14	Psalm 68 Genesis 4. 1-16, 25-26 Matthew 22. 15-33	Psalm [84;] 85 Genesis 6. 1-10 Matthew 22. 34-end

THE SECOND SUNDAY *of* EPIPHANY

DATE	COLLECT & PC	PRINCIPAL SERVICE
Sunday 19 January	21 & 22	Isaiah 62. 1-5 Psalm 36. 5-10 1 Corinthians 12. 1-11 John 2. 1-11

18-25 January: Week of Prayers for Christian Unity *continued*.

Monday 20 January	Tuesday 21 January † Agnes	Wednesday 22 January
DAILY EUCHARIST		
Collect & PC 21 & 22 Hebrews 5. 1-10 Psalm 110. 1-4 Mark 2. 18-22	Collect & PC 21 & 22 Hebrews 6. 10-end Psalm 111 Mark 2. 23-end	Collect & PC 21 & 22 Hebrews 7. 1-3, 15-17 Psalm 110. 1-4 Mark 3. 1-6
Morning Prayer		
Psalm [145;] 146 Amos 6 1 Corinthians 6. 1-11	Psalm 132; [147. 1-12] Amos 7 1 Corinthians 6. 12-end	Psalm 81; [147. 13-end] Amos 8 1 Corinthians 7. 1-24
Evening Prayer		
Psalm 71 Genesis 6.11 – 7.10 Matthew 24. 1-14	Psalm 89. 1-37 Genesis 7. 11-end Matthew 24. 15-28	Psalm 97; [98] Genesis 8. 1-14 Matthew 24. 29-end

Advent 2024 - Kingdom 2025

THIRD SERVICE	SECOND SERVICE	Notes
Psalm 145. 1-13 Isaiah 49. 1-7 Acts 16. 11-15	Psalm 96 1 Samuel 3. 1-20 Ephesians 4. 1-16 *If the Second Service is a Eucharist, the Gospel is:* John 1. 29-42	1984 BCP page 53. * For the replaced readings, see page 115. † For weekday commemorations see page 126.

	† Francis de Sales	* The Conversion of Paul, Apostle
Thursday 23 January	Friday 24 January	Saturday 25 January
DAILY EUCHARIST		
Collect & PC 21 & 22 Hebrews 7.25 - 8.6 Psalm 40. 7-10 Mark 3. 7-12	Collect & PC 21 & 22 Hebrews 8. 6-end Psalm 85. 7-end Mark 3. 13-19	Collect 153 & PC 363 / 365 Jeremiah 1. 4-10 Psalm 67 Acts 9. 1-22 Matthew 19. [24-26,] 27-30 *or* Acts 9. 1-22 Psalm 67 Galatians 1. 11-16a Matthew 19. [24-26,] 27-30
Morning Prayer		
Psalm 76; [148] Amos 9 1 Corinthians 7. 25-end	Psalm 27; [149] Hosea 1.1 – 2.1 1 Corinthians 8	Psalm 66 Ezekiel 3. 22-27 Philippians 3. 1-14
Evening Prayer		
Psalm [99; 100;] 111 Genesis 8.15 – 9.7 Matthew 25. 1-13	Psalm 73 Genesis 9. 8-19 Matthew 25. 14-30	Psalm 119. 41-56 Sirach 39. 1-10 *or* Isaiah 56. 1-8 Colossians 1.24 – 2.7
	... on the eve of The Conversion of Paul: *Psalm 149: Isaiah 49. 1-13: Acts 22. 3-16*	

Year C - Weekdays 1

THE THIRD SUNDAY *of* EPIPHANY

DATE	COLLECT & PC	PRINCIPAL SERVICE
Sunday 26 January (†) World Leprosy Day	23 & 24	Nehemiah 8. 1-3, 5-6, 8-10 Psalm 19 *or* 19. 1-6 1 Corinthians 12. 12-31a Luke 4. 14-21

Holocaust Memorial Day		
† John Chrysostom	† Thomas Aquinas	
Monday 27 January	Tuesday 28 January	Wednesday 29 January
DAILY EUCHARIST		
Collect & PC 23 & 24 Hebrews 9. 15, 24-28 Psalm 98 Mark 3. 19b-30	Collect & PC 23 & 24 Hebrews 10. 1-10 Psalm 40. 1-11 Mark 3. 31-35	Collect & PC 23 & 24 Hebrews 10. 11-18 Psalm 110. 1-4 Mark 4. 1-20
Morning Prayer		
Psalm [40;] 108 Hosea 2.18 – *end of* 3 1 Corinthians 9. 15-end	Psalm [34;] 36 Hosea 4. 1-16 1 Corinthians 10. 1-13	Psalm [45;] 46 Hosea 5. 1-7 1 Corinthians 10.14 – 11.1
Evening Prayer		
Psalm 138; [144] Genesis 11.27 – 12.9 Matthew 26. 1-16	Psalm 145 Genesis 13. 2-end Matthew 26. 17-35	Psalm [21;] 29 Genesis 14 Matthew 26. 36-46

Advent 2024 - Kingdom 2025

THIRD SERVICE	SECOND SERVICE	Notes
Psalm 113 Deuteronomy 30. 11-15 3 John 1. 5-8	Psalm 33 Numbers 9. 15-23 1 Corinthians 7. 17-24 *If the Second Service is a Eucharist, the Gospel is:* Mark 1. 21-28	1984 BCP page 56. † For weekday commemorations see page 126 & 127.

		† Brigid *or* Bride
Thursday 30 January	Friday 30 January	Saturday 1 February
	DAILY EUCHARIST	
Collect & PC 23 & 24 Hebrews 10. 19-25 Psalm 24. 1-6 Mark 4. 21-25	Collect & PC 23 & 24 Hebrews 10. 32-39 Psalm 37. 1-7, 23, 24 Mark 4. 26-34	Collect & PC 23 & 24 Hebrews 11. 1, 2, 8-19 Psalm 89. 19-29 Mark 4. 35-41
	Morning Prayer	
Psalm 47; [48] Hosea 5.8 – 6.6 1 Corinthians 11. 2-16	Psalm [61;] 65 Hosea 6.7 – 7.2 1 Corinthians 11. 17-end	Psalm 68 Hosea 8 1 Corinthians 12. 1-11
	Evening Prayer	
Psalm 24; [33] Genesis 15 Matthew 26. 47-56	Psalm 67; [77] Genesis 16 Matthew 26. 57-end	Psalm 72; [76] Genesis 17. 1-22 Matthew 27. 1-10
		... on the eve of The Presentation: *Psalm 118: 1 Samuel 1. 19b-28: Hebrews 4. 11-16*

THE PRESENTATION OF CHRIST (Candlemas)

DATE	COLLECT & PC	PRINCIPAL SERVICE
Sunday 2 February	27 & 28	Malachi 3. 1-5 Psalm 24. [1-6,] 7-10 Hebrews 2. 14-18 Luke 2. 22-40

† The Saints, Martyrs and Missionaries *of* Europe *or* Seiriol	† Manche Masemola	
Monday 3 February	**Tuesday 4 February**	**Wednesday 5 February**
DAILY EUCHARIST		
Collect & PC 25 & 26 Hebrews 11. 32-40 Psalm 31. 19-24 Mark 5. 1-20	Collect & PC 25 & 26 Hebrews 12. 1-4 Psalm 22. 22-31 Mark 5. 21-43	Collect & PC 25 & 26 Hebrews 12. 4-7, 11-15 Psalm 103. 1, 2, 13-18 Mark 6. 1-6
Morning Prayer		
Psalm 1; [2; 3] Hosea 9 1 Corinthians 12. 12-end	Psalm 5; [6; 8] Hosea 10 1 Corinthians 13	Psalm 119. 1-32 Hosea 11. 1-11 1 Corinthians 14. 1-19
Evening Prayer		
Psalm 4; [7] Genesis 18. 1-15 Matthew 27. 11-26	Psalm 9; [10] Genesis 18. 16-end Matthew 27. 27-44	Psalm 11; [12; 13] Genesis 19. 1-3, 12-29 Matthew 27. 45-56

Advent 2024 - Kingdom 2025

THIRD SERVICE	SECOND SERVICE	Notes
Psalm 42; 43; 48 Exodus 13. 1-16 Romans 12. 1-5	Psalm 122; 132 Haggai 2. 1-9 John 2. 18-22	1984 BCP page 58 † For weekday commemorations see page 127.

Thursday 6 February	Friday 7 February	Saturday 8 February
DAILY EUCHARIST		
Collect & PC 25 & 26 Hebrews 12. 18-24 Psalm 48. 1-3, 8-10 Mark 6. 7-13	Collect & PC 25 & 26 Hebrews 13. 1-8 Psalm 27. 1-10 Mark 6. 14-29	Collect & PC 25 & 26 Hebrews 13. 9-17, 20, 21 Psalm 23 Mark 6. 30-34
Morning Prayer		
Psalm [14;] 15; [16] Hosea 11.12 – *end of* 12 1 Corinthians 14. 20-end	Psalm [17;] 19 Hosea 13. 1-14 1 Corinthians 16. 1-9	Psalm [20; 21;] 23 Hosea 14 1 Corinthians 16. 10-end
Evening Prayer		
Psalm 18 Genesis 21. 1-21 Matthew 27. 57-end	Psalm 22 Genesis 22. 1-19 Matthew 28. 1-15	Psalm 24; [25] Genesis 23 Matthew 28. 16-end

Year C - Weekdays 1

THE FOURTH SUNDAY *before* LENT		
DATE	COLLECT & PC	PRINCIPAL SERVICE
Sunday 9 February (†)	31 & 32	Isaiah 6. 1-8, [9-13] Psalm 138 1 Corinthians 15. 1-11 Luke 5. 1-11
Racial Justice Sunday		

Monday 10 February	Tuesday 11 February	Wednesday 12 February
DAILY EUCHARIST		
Collect & PC 31 & 32 Genesis 1. 1-19 Psalm 104. 1-12, 24 Mark 6. 53-56	Collect & PC 31 & 32 Genesis 1.20 – 2.4a Psalm 8 Mark 7. 1-13	Collect & PC 31 & 32 Genesis 2. 4b-9, 15-17 Psalm 104. 24, 27-30 Mark 7. 14-23
Morning Prayer		
Psalm [27;] 30 Joel 1. 1-14 John 15. 1-11	Psalm [32;] 36 Joel 1. 15-end John 15. 12-17	Psalm 34 Joel 2. 1-17 John 15. 18-end
Evening Prayer		
Psalm [26;] 28; [29] Leviticus 19. 1-18, 30-end 1 Timothy 1. 1-17	Psalm 33 Leviticus 23. 1-22 1 Timothy 1.18 – *end of* 2	Psalm 119. 33-56 Leviticus 23. 23-end 1 Timothy 3

Advent 2024 - Kingdom 2025

THIRD SERVICE	SECOND SERVICE	Notes
Psalm 3; 4 Jeremiah 26. 1-16 Acts 3. 1-10	Psalm [1;] 2 Wisdom 6. 1-21 *or* Hosea 1 Colossians 3. 1-22 *If the Second Service is a Eucharist, the Gospel is:* Matthew 5. 13-20	1984 BCP page 63 † For weekday commemorations see page 127.

† Cyril *and* Methodius

Thursday 13 February	Friday 14 February	Saturday 15 February
\multicolumn{3}{c}{DAILY EUCHARIST}		
Collect & PC 31 & 32 Genesis 2. 18-25 Psalm 128 Mark 7. 24-30	Collect & PC 31 & 32 Genesis 3. 1-8 Psalm 32. 1-7 Mark 7. 31-37	Collect & PC 31 & 32 Genesis 3. 9-24 Psalm 90. 1-12 Mark 8. 1-10
	Morning Prayer	
Psalm 37 Joel 2. 18-27 John 16. 1-15	Psalm 31 Joel 2. 28-end John 16. 16-22	Psalm [41;] 42; [43] Joel 3. 1-3, 9-end John 16. 23-end
	Evening Prayer	
Psalm [39;] 40 Leviticus 24. 1-9 1 Timothy 4	Psalm 35 Leviticus 25. 1-24 1 Timothy 5. 1-16	Psalm [45;] 46 Numbers 6. 1-5, 21-end 1 Timothy 5. 17-end

Year C - Weekdays 1

THE THIRD SUNDAY *before* LENT

DATE	COLLECT & PC	PRINCIPAL SERVICE
Sunday 16 February	33 & 34	Jeremiah 17. 5-10 Psalm 1 1 Corinthians 15. 12-20 Luke 6. 17-26

Monday 17 February	† John of Fiesole and Andrei Rublev Tuesday 18 February	† Thomas Burgess Wednesday 19 February
\multicolumn{3}{c}{**DAILY EUCHARIST**}		
Collect & PC 33 & 34 Genesis 4. 1-15, 25 Psalm 50. 7-23 Mark 8. 11-13	Collect & PC 33 & 34 Genesis 6. 5-8; 7. 1-5, 10 Psalm 29 Mark 8. 14-21	Collect & PC 33 & 34 Genesis 8. 6-13, 20-22 Psalm 116. 12-19 Mark 8. 22-26
	Morning Prayer	
Psalm 44 Ecclesiastes 1 John 17. 1-5	Psalm 48; [52] Ecclesiastes 2 John 17. 6-19	Psalm 119. 57-80 Ecclesiastes 3. 1-15 John 17. 20-end
	Evening Prayer	
Psalm 47; [49] Genesis 24. 1-28 1 Timothy 6. 1-10	Psalm 50 Genesis 24. 29-end 1 Timothy 6. 11-end	Psalm 59; [60; 67] Genesis 25. 7-11, 19-end 2 Timothy 1. 1-14

Advent 2024 - Kingdom 2025

THIRD SERVICE	SECOND SERVICE	Notes
Psalm 7 Jeremiah 30. 1-3, 10-22 Acts 6	Psalm [5;] 6 Wisdom 11.21 – 12.11 *or* Hosea 10. 1-8, 12 Galatians 4. 8-20 *If the Second Service is a Eucharist, the Gospel is:* **Matthew 5. 21-37**	1984 BCP page 66 (Septuagesima). † For weekday commemorations see page 128.

† The Saints, Martyrs and Missionaries *of* Africa

Thursday 20 February	Friday 21 February	Saturday 22 February
DAILY EUCHARIST		
Collect & PC 33 & 34 Genesis 9. 1-13 Psalm 102. 15-22 Mark 8. 27-33	Collect & PC 33 & 34 Genesis 11. 1-9 Psalm 33. 6-18 Mark 8.34 – 9.1	Collect & PC 33 & 34 Hebrews 11. 1-7 Psalm 145. 1-4, 10-13 Mark 9. 2-13
Morning Prayer		
Psalm [56;] 57; [63] Eccles. 3.16 – *end of* 4 John 18. 1-11	Psalm 51; [54] Ecclesiastes 5 John 18. 12-27	Psalm 68 Ecclesiastes 6 John 18. 28-end
Evening Prayer		
Psalm [61;] 62; [64] Genesis 26.34 – 27.40 2 Timothy 1.15 – 2.13	Psalm 38 Genesis 27.41 – *end of* 28 2 Timothy 2. 14-end	Psalm [65;] 66 Genesis 29. 1-30 2 Timothy 3

THE SECOND SUNDAY *before* LENT: CREATION SUNDAY

DATE	COLLECT & PC	PRINCIPAL SERVICE
Sunday 23 February (†)	35 & 36	Genesis 2. 4b-9, 15-25 Psalm 65 Revelation 4 Luke 8. 22-25

Monday 24 February	Tuesday 25 February	Wednesday 26 February
DAILY EUCHARIST		
Collect & PC 35 & 36 Sirach 1. 1-10 Psalm 93 Mark 9. 14-29	Collect & PC 35 & 36 Sirach 2. 1-11 Psalm 37. 3-6, 26-28 Mark 9. 30-37	Collect & PC 35 & 36 Sirach 4. 11-19 Psalm 119. 161-168 Mark 9. 38-41
Morning Prayer		
Psalm 71 Ecclesiastes 7. 1-14 John 19. 1-16	Psalm 73 Ecclesiastes 7. 15-end John 19. 17-30	Psalm 77 Ecclesiastes 8 John 19. 31-end
Evening Prayer		
Psalm 72; [75] Genesis 29.31 – 30.24 2 Timothy 4. 1-8	Psalm 74 Genesis 31. 1-24 2 Timothy 4. 9-end	Psalm 119. 81-104 Genesis 31.25 – 32.2 Titus 1

Advent 2024 - Kingdom 2025

THIRD SERVICE	SECOND SERVICE	Notes
Psalm 104. 1-25 Job 28. 1-11 Acts 14. 8-17	Psalm 147 *or* 147. 12-20 Genesis 1.1 – 2.3 Matthew 6. 25-34	1984 BCP page 69 (Sexagesima). *For the replaced readings, see page 115. † For weekday commemorations see page 128.

† George Herbert and all Pastors		*David, Bishop of St Davids, Patron Saint of Wales
Thursday 27 February	**Friday 28 February**	**Saturday 1 March**
DAILY EUCHARIST		
Collect & PC 35 & 36 Sirach 5. 1-8 Psalm 1 Mark 9. 42-50	Collect & PC 35 & 36 Sirach 6. 5-17 Psalm 119. 17-24 Mark 10. 1-12	Collect & PC 168 & 169 Sirach 15. 1-6 *or* Jeremiah 1. 4-10 Psalm 16. 3, 5-8 1 Thessalonians 2. 2b-12 Matthew 16. 24-27
Morning Prayer		
Psalm 78. 1-39 Ecclesiastes 9 John 20. 1-10	Psalm 55 Ecclesiastes 11. 1-8 John 20. 11-18	Psalm 112 Wisdom 5. 1-16 *or* 2 Samuel 23. 1-4 Hebrews 11. 8-16
Evening Prayer		
Psalm 78. 40-end Genesis 32. 3-30 Titus 2	Psalm 69 Genesis 33. 1-17 Titus 3	Psalm 92 Ezekiel 2. 1-7 1 Timothy 4. 1-8
	... on the eve of David: Psalm 28. 1, 2, 6-9: Exodus 19. 3-6a: Revelation 5. 6-10	

Year C - Weekdays 1

THE SUNDAY *before* LENT: TRANSFIGURATION SUNDAY

DATE	COLLECT & PC	PRINCIPAL SERVICE
Sunday 2 March (†)	37 & 38	Exodus 34. 29-35 Psalm 99 2 Corinthians 3.12 – 4.2 Luke 9. 28-36, [37-43]

Monday 3 March	Tuesday 4 March	ASH WEDNESDAY (†) Wednesday 5 March
DAILY EUCHARIST		**PRINCIPAL SERVICE**
Collect & PC 37 & 38 Sirach 17. 24-29 Psalm 32. 1-7 Mark 10. 17-27	Collect & PC 37 & 38 Sirach 35. 1-12 Psalm 50. 7-15 Mark 10. 28-31	Collect & PC 39 & 40 Joel 2. 1-2, 12-17 *or* Isaiah 58. 1-12 Psalm 51. 1-17 2 Corinthians 5.20b – 6.10 Matthew 6. 1-6, 16-21 *or* John 8. 1-11
Morning Prayer		**THIRD SERVICE**
Psalm 80; [82] Jeremiah 1 John 3. 1-21	Psalm [87;] 89. 1-18 Jeremiah 2. 1-13 John 3. 22-end	Psalm 38 Daniel 9. 3-6, 17-19 1 Timothy 6. 6-19
Evening Prayer		**SECOND SERVICE**
Psalm [85;] 86 Genesis 37. 1-11 Galatians 1	Psalm 89.19-end Genesis 37. 12-end Galatians 2. 1-10	Psalm 102 *or* 102. 1-17 Isaiah 1. 10-18 Luke 15. 11-32

Advent 2024 - Kingdom 2025

THIRD SERVICE	SECOND SERVICE	Notes
Psalm 2 Exodus 33. 17-23 1 John 3. 1-3	Psalm 89. 1-4, [5-12,] 13-18 Exodus 3. 1-6 John 12. 27-36a	1984 BCP page 72 (Quinquagesima). † For weekday commemorations see page 129.

Women's World Day of Prayer

† Perpetua, Felicity and their Companions

Thursday 6 March	Friday 7 March	Saturday 8 March
DAILY EUCHARIST		
Collect & PC 37 & 38 Deuteronomy 30. 15-20 Psalm 1 Luke 9. 18-25	Collect & PC 37 & 38 Isaiah 58. 1-9a Psalm 51. 1-4, 16, 17 Matthew 9. 14-17	Collect & PC 37 & 38 Isaiah 58. 9b-14 Psalm 86. 1-6 Luke 5. 27-32
Morning Prayer		
Psalm 77 Jeremiah 2. 14-32 John 4. 1-26	Psalm 3; [7] Jeremiah 3. 6-22 John 4. 27-42	Psalm 71 Jeremiah 4. 1-18 John 4. 43-end
Evening Prayer		
Psalm 74 Genesis 39 Galatians 2. 11-end	Psalm 31 Genesis 40 Galatians 3. 1-14	Psalm 73 Genesis 41. 1-24 Galatians 3. 15-22

Year C - Weekdays 1

THE FIRST SUNDAY *of* LENT

DATE	COLLECT & PC	PRINCIPAL SERVICE
Sunday 9 March (†)	42 & 43	Deuteronomy 26. 1-11 Psalm 91. 1, 2, 9-16 *or* 91. 1-11 Romans 10. 8b-13 Luke 4. 1-13

Monday 10 March	Tuesday 11 March	Ember Day Wednesday 12 March
DAILY EUCHARIST		
Collect & PC 42 & 43 Leviticus 19. 1, 2, 11-18 Psalm 19. 7-14 Matthew 25. 31-46	Collect & PC 42 & 43 Isaiah 55. 10, 11 Psalm 34. 1-8, [15-22] Matthew 6. 7-15	Collect & PC 351 & 352 Ember set 1,2 *or* 3. See page 154.
Morning Prayer		
Psalm [10;] 11 Jeremiah 4. 19-end John 5. 1-18	Psalm 44 Jeremiah 5. 1-19 John 5. 19-29	Psalm 6; [17] Jeremiah 5. 20-end John 5. 30-end
Evening Prayer		
Psalm [12;] 13; [14] Genesis 41. 25-45 Galatians 3.23 – 4.7	Psalm [46;] 49 Genesis 41.46 – 42.5 Galatians 4. 8-20	Psalm [9;] 28 Genesis 42. 6-17 Galatians 4.21 – 5.1

Advent 2024 - Kingdom 2025

THIRD SERVICE	SECOND SERVICE	Notes
Psalm 50. 1-15 Micah 6. 1-8 Luke 5. 27-39	Psalm 119. 73-88 Jonah 3 Luke 18. 9-14	1984 BCP page 77.

Thursday 13 March	Ember Day Friday 14 March	Ember Day Saturday 15 March
DAILY EUCHARIST		
Collect & PC 42 & 43 Esther 14. 1, 3-5, 12-14 Psalm 138 Matthew 7. 7-12	Collect & PC 351 & 352 Ember set 1,2 *or* 3. See page 154.	Collect & PC 351 & 352 Ember set 1,2 *or* 3. See page 154.
Morning Prayer		
Psalm 42; [43] Jeremiah 6. 9-21 John 6. 1-15	Psalm 22 Jeremiah 6. 22-end John 6. 16-27	Psalm [59;] 63 Jeremiah 7. 1-20 John 6. 27-40
Evening Prayer		
Psalm [137; 138;] 142 Genesis 42. 18-28 Galatians 5. 2-15	Psalm [54;] 55 Genesis 42. 29-end Galatians 5. 16-end	Psalm 4; [16] Genesis 43. 1-15 Galatians 6

Year C - Weekdays 1

THE SECOND SUNDAY of LENT

DATE	COLLECT & PC	PRINCIPAL SERVICE
Sunday 16 March	44 & 45	Genesis 15. 1-12, 17, 18 Psalm 27 Philippians 3.17 - 4.1 Luke 13. 31-35

† Patrick	† Cyril of Jerusalem	* Joseph *of* Nazareth
Monday 17 March	Tuesday 18 March	Wednesday 19 March

DAILY EUCHARIST

Collect & PC 44 & 45	Collect & PC 44 & 45	Collect & PC 174 & 389
Daniel 9. 3-10	Isaiah 1. 10-20	2 Samuel 7. 10-16
Psalm 79	Psalm 50. 7-15	Psalm 89. [27-34,] 35-37
Luke 6. 36-38	Matthew 23. 1-12	Romans 4. 13-18
		Matthew 1. 18-25

Morning Prayer

Psalm [26;] 32	Psalm 50	Psalm 25
Jeremiah 7. 21-end	Jeremiah 8. 1-15	Isaiah 11. 1-10
John 6. 41-51	John 6. 52-59	Matthew 13. 54-58

Evening Prayer

Psalm [70;] 74	Psalm 52; [53; 54]	Psalm 1; 112
Genesis 43. 16-end	Genesis 44. 1-17	Genesis 50. 22-26
Hebrews 1	Hebrews 2. 1-9	Matthew 2. 13-23

... on the eve of Joseph:
Psalm 132: Hosea 11. 1-9: Luke 2. 41-52

Advent 2024 - Kingdom 2025

THIRD SERVICE	SECOND SERVICE	Notes
Psalm 119. 161-176 Genesis 17. 1-7, 15-16 Romans 11. 13-24	Psalm 135 Jeremiah 22. 1-9, 13-17 Luke 14. 27-33	1984 BCP page 80. * For the replaced readings, see page 115. † For weekday commemorations see page 129 & 130.

† Cuthbert	† Thomas Cranmer, Hugh Latimer, Nicholas Ridley and Robert Ferrar	
Thursday 20 March	**Friday 21 March**	**Saturday 22 March**
	DAILY EUCHARIST	
Collect & PC 44 & 45 Jeremiah 17. 5-10 Psalm 1 Luke 16. 19-31	Collect & PC 168 & 169 Genesis 37. 3, 4, 12-28 Psalm 17. 1-8 Matthew 21. 33-46	Collect & PC 44 & 45 Micah 7. 14-20 Psalm 103. 1-12 Luke 15. 1-3, 11-32
	Morning Prayer	
Psalm 34 Jeremiah 9. 12-24 John 7. 1-13	Psalm [40;] 41 Jeremiah 10. 1-16 John 7. 14-24	Psalm [3;] 25 Jeremiah 10. 17-24 John 7. 25-36
	Evening Prayer	
Psalm 71 Genesis 45. 1-15 Hebrews 3. 1-6	Psalm 6; [38] Genesis 45. 16-end Hebrews 3. 7-end	Psalm 23; [27] Genesis 46. 1-7, 28-end Hebrews 4. 1-13

THE THIRD SUNDAY *of* LENT

DATE	COLLECT & PC	PRINCIPAL SERVICE
Sunday 23 March	46 & 47	Isaiah 55. 1-9 Psalm 63. 1-8 1 Corinthians 10. 1-13 Luke 13. 1-9

† Oscar Romero Monday 24 March	*The Annunciation of Our Lord to the Blessed Virgin Mary Tuesday 25 March	Wednesday 26 March
DAILY EUCHARIST		
Collect & PC 46 & 47 2 Kings 5. 1-15a Psalm 42. 1, 2: 43.1-4 Luke 4. 24-30	Collect & PC 177 & 8 Isaiah 7. 10-14 Psalm 45 *or* 40. 5-10 Hebrews 10. 4-10 Luke 1. 26-38	Collect & PC 46 & 47 Deuteronomy 4. 1, 5-10 Psalm 147. 12-20 Matthew 5. 17-20
Morning Prayer		
Psalm 5; [7] Jeremiah 11. 1-17 John 7. 37-52	Psalm 111; 113 1 Samuel 2. 1-10 Romans 5. 12-21	Psalm 38 Jeremiah 13. 1-11 John 8. 12-30
Evening Prayer		
Psalm [11;] 17 Genesis 47. 1-27 Hebrews 4.14 – 5.10	Psalm 131; 146 Isaiah 52. 1-12 Hebrews 2. 5-18	Psalm [36;] 39 Genesis 49. 1-32 Hebrews 6. 13-end
... on the eve of the Annunciation: **Psalm 85: Wisdom 9. 1-12 or Genesis 3. 8-15: Galatians 4. 1-5**		

Advent 2024 - Kingdom 2025

THIRD SERVICE	SECOND SERVICE	Notes
Psalm 26; 28 Deuteronomy 6. 4-9 John 17. 1a, 11b-19	Psalm 12; 13 Genesis 28. 10-19a John 1. 35-51	1984 BCP page 83. * For the replaced readings, see page 116. † For weekday commemorations see page 130.

		† Woolos
Thursday 27 March	**Friday 28 March**	**Saturday 29 March**
DAILY EUCHARIST		
Collect & PC 46 & 47 Jeremiah 7. 21-28 Psalm 95. 1-9 Luke 11. 14-23	Collect & PC 46 & 47 Hosea 14. 1-9 Psalm 81 Mark 12. 28-34	Collect & PC 46 & 47 Hosea 5.13 – 6.6 Psalm 51. 1-4, 16-19 Luke 18. 9-14
Morning Prayer		
Psalm 56; [57] Jeremiah 14 John 8. 31-47	Psalm 22 Jeremiah 15. 10-end John 8. 48-end	Psalm 31 Jeremiah 16.10 – 17.4 John 9. 1-17
Evening Prayer		
Psalm 59; [60] Genesis 49.33 – *end of* 50 Hebrews 7. 1-10	Psalm 69 Exodus 1. 1-14 Hebrews 7. 11-end	Psalm 116; [130] Exodus 1.22 – 2.10 Hebrews 8

Year C - Weekdays 1

THE FOURTH SUNDAY *of* LENT / LENT 4 *as* MOTHERING SUNDAY

DATE	COLLECT & PC	PRINCIPAL SERVICE
Sunday 30 March	48 & 49	Joshua 5. 9-12 Psalm 32 2 Corinthians 5. 16-21 Luke 15. 1-3, 11b-32
Mothering Sunday	50 & 49	Exodus 2. 1-10 *or* 1 Samuel 1. 20-28 Psalm 34. 11-20 *or* Psalm 127. 1-4 2 Corinthians 1. 3-7 *or* Colossians 3. 12-17 Luke 2. 33-35 *or* John 19. 25-27

Monday 31 March	Tuesday 1 April	Wednesday 2 April
DAILY EUCHARIST		
Collect & PC 48 & 49 Isaiah 65. 17-21 Psalm 30 John 4. 43-54	Collect & PC 48 & 49 Ezekiel 47. 1-9, 12 Psalm 46 John 5. 1-18	Collect & PC 48 & 49 Isaiah 49. 8-15 Psalm 145. 8-14 John 5. 19-30
Morning Prayer		
Psalm [70;] 77 Jeremiah 17. 5-18 John 9. 18-end	Psalm [54;] 79 Jeremiah 18. 1-12 John 10. 1-10	Psalm [63;] 90 Jeremiah 18. 13-end John 10. 11-21
Evening Prayer		
Psalm 25; [28] Exodus 2. 11-22 Hebrews 9. 1-14	Psalm 80; [82] Exodus 2.23 – 3.20 Hebrews 9. 15-end	Psalm [52;] 91 Exodus 4. 1-23 Hebrews 10. 1-18

Advent 2024 - Kingdom 2025

THIRD SERVICE	SECOND SERVICE	Notes
Psalm 84; 85 Genesis 37. 3-4, 12-36 1 Peter 2. 16-25	Psalm 30 Prayer of Manasseh *or* Isaiah 40.27 – 41.13 2 Timothy 4. 1-18 *If the Second Service is a Eucharist, the Gospel is:* John 11. 17-44	1984 BCP page 85.

Thursday 3 April	Friday 4 April	Saturday 5 April
DAILY EUCHARIST		
Collect & PC 48 & 49 Exodus 32. 7-14 Psalm 103. 1-12 John 5. 31-47	Collect & PC 48 & 49 Wisdom 2. 1a, 12-22 Psalm 34. 15-22 John 7. 1, 2, 10, 25-30	Collect & PC 48 & 49 Jeremiah 11. 18-20 Psalm 7. 1, 2, 8-11 John 7. 40-53
Morning Prayer		
Psalm [53;] 86 Jeremiah 19. 1-13 John 10. 22-end	Psalm 102 Jeremiah 19.14 – 20.6 John 11. 1-16	Psalm 32 Jeremiah 20. 7-end John 11. 17-27
Evening Prayer		
Psalm 94 Exodus 4.27 – 6.1 Hebrews 10. 19-25	Psalm [13;] 16 Exodus 6. 2-13 Hebrews 10. 26-end	Psalm 140; [141; 142] Exodus 7. 8-end Hebrews 11. 1-16

Year C - Weekdays 1

THE FIFTH SUNDAY *of* LENT: PASSION SUNDAY

DATE	COLLECT & PC	PRINCIPAL SERVICE
Sunday 6 April	51 & 52	Isaiah 43. 16-21 Psalm 126 Philippians 3. 4b-14 John 12. 1-8

† Brynach	† Griffith Jones	† Saints, Martyrs and Missionaries *of* South America *or* Dietrich Bonhoeffer
Monday 7 April	**Tuesday 8 April**	**Wednesday 9 April**
DAILY EUCHARIST		
Collect & PC 51 & 52 Susanna 1. 1-9, 15-17, 19-30, 33-62 *or* Susanna 1. 41c-62 Psalm 23 John 8. 1-11	Collect & PC 51 & 52 Numbers 21. 4-9 Psalm 102. 1, 2, 15-22 John 8. 21-30	Collect & PC 51 & 52 Daniel 3. 13-28 Psalm 24. 1-6 John 8. 31-47
Morning Prayer		
Psalm 73; [121] Jeremiah 21. 1-10 John 11. 28-44	Psalm 35; [123] Jeremiah 22. 1-5, 13-19 John 11. 45-end	Psalm 55; [124] Jeremiah 22.20 – 23.8 John 12. 1-11
Evening Prayer		
Psalm 26; [27] Exodus 8. 1-19 Hebrews 11. 17-31	Psalm 61; [64] Exodus 8. 20-end Hebrews 11.32 – 12.2	Psalm [56;] 62 Exodus 9. 1-12 Hebrews 12. 3-13

Advent 2024 - Kingdom 2025

Colour Variation: Passion Red - *Passiontide begins*		
THIRD SERVICE	**SECOND SERVICE**	**Notes**
Psalm 111; 112 Isaiah 35. 1-10 Romans 7.21 – 8.4	Psalm 35 *or* 35. 1-9 2 Chronicles 35. 1-6, 10-16 Luke 22. 1-13	1984 BCP page 88 † For weekday commemorations see page 130 & 131.

† George Augustus Selwyn

Thursday 10 April	Friday 11 April	Saturday 12 April
DAILY EUCHARIST		
Collect & PC 51 & 52 Genesis 17. 3-9 Psalm 105. 1-9 John 8. 51-59	Collect & PC 51 & 52 Jeremiah 20. 7-13 Psalm 18. 1-6 John 10. 31-42	Collect & PC 51 & 52 Ezekiel 37. 21b-28 Psalm 121 John 11. 45-57
Morning Prayer		
Psalm 40; [125] Jeremiah 23. 9-32 John 12. 12-19	Psalm 22; [126] Jeremiah 24 John 12. 20-36a	Psalm 23; [127] Jeremiah 25. 1-14 John 12. 36b-end
Evening Prayer		
Psalm [42;] 43 Exodus 9. 13-end Hebrews 12. 14-end	Psalm 31 Exodus 10 Hebrews 13. 1-16	Psalm [128; 129;] 130 Exodus 11 Hebrews 13. 17-end

THE SIXTH SUNDAY OF LENT: PALM SUNDAY

DATE	COLLECT & PC	PRINCIPAL SERVICE	
Sunday 13 April	53 & 54	*Liturgy of the Palms:* Luke 19. 28-40 Psalm 118. [1, 2,] 19-29 Philippians 2. 5-11 Luke 22.14 – 23.56 *or* Luke 23. 1-49	*Liturgy of the Passion:* Isaiah 50. 4-9a Psalm 31. 9-16, [17, 18] Philippians 2. 5-11 Luke 22.14 – 23.56 *or* Luke 23. 1-49

MONDAY IN HOLY WEEK

DATE	COLLECT & PC	PRINCIPAL SERVICE
Monday 14 April	53 & 54	Isaiah 42. 1-9 Psalm 36. 5-11 Hebrews 9. 11-15 John 12. 1-11

TUESDAY IN HOLY WEEK

DATE	COLLECT & PC	PRINCIPAL SERVICE
Tuesday 15 April (†)	53 & 54	Isaiah 49. 1-7 Psalm 71. 1-8, [9-14] 1 Corinthians 1. 18-31 John 12. 20-36

WEDNESDAY IN HOLY WEEK

DATE	COLLECT & PC	PRINCIPAL SERVICE
Wednesday 16 April	53 & 54	Isaiah 50. 4-9a Psalm 70 Hebrews 12. 1-3 John 13. 21-32

Advent 2024 - Kingdom 2025

Colour Variation: Purple can be used until Easter Day.		
THIRD SERVICE	SECOND SERVICE	Notes
Psalm 61; 62 Zechariah 9. 9 -12 1 Corinthians 2. 1-12	Psalm 69. 1-18 Isaiah 5. 1-7 Luke 20. 9-19	1984 BCP page 91.

Colour Variation: Purple can be used until Easter Day.		
THIRD SERVICE	SECOND SERVICE	Notes
Psalm 25 Lamentations 2. 8-19 Colossians 1. 18-23	Psalm 41 Lamentations 1. 1-12a Luke 22. 1-23	1984 BCP page 95.

Colour Variation: Purple can be used until Easter Day.		
THIRD SERVICE	SECOND SERVICE	Notes
Psalm 55. 12-22 Lamentations 3. 40-51 Galatians 6. 11-18	Psalm 27 Lamentations 3. 1-18 Luke 22. [24-38,] 39-53	1984 BCP page 101. (†) For weekday commemorations see page 131.

Colour Variation: Purple can be used until Easter Day.		
THIRD SERVICE	SECOND SERVICE	Notes
Psalm 88 Isaiah 63. 1-9 Revelation 14.18 – 15.4	Psalm 102 *or* 102. 1-17 Wisdom 1.16 – 2.1; 2. 12-22 *or* Jeremiah 11. 18-20 Luke 22. 54-71	1984 BCP page 105.

MAUNDY THURSDAY		
DATE	COLLECT & PC	PRINCIPAL SERVICE
Thursday 17 April	55 & 56 53 *(Services other than the Eucharist.)*	*Eucharist:* Exodus 12. 1-4, [5-10,] 11-14 Psalm 116. 1, 2, 12-19 *or* 116. 12-19 1 Corinthians 11. 23-26 John 13. 1-17, 31b-35

GOOD FRIDAY		
DATE	COLLECT & PC	PRINCIPAL SERVICE
Friday 18 April	57 & 58	Isaiah 52.13 – 53.12 Psalm 22 *or* 22. 1-11 *or* 22. 1-21 Hebrews 10. 16-25 *or* 4. 14-16; 5. 7-9 John 18.1 – 19.42

EASTER EVE		
DATE	COLLECT & PC	PRINCIPAL SERVICE
Saturday 19 April	59	*Services other than the Easter Vigil.* Job 14. 1-14 *or* Lamentations 3. 1-9, 19-24 Psalm 31. 1-4, 15-16 *or* 31. 1-5 1 Peter 4. 1-8 Matthew 27. 57-66 *or* John 19. 38-42

EASTER VIGIL

A minimum of three Old Testament readings should be chosen.
The readings from Exodus 14, Romans and the Gospel should always be used.
Genesis 1.1 – 2.4a *with* Psalm 136. 1-9, 23-26
Genesis 7. 1-5, 11-18; 8. 6-18; 9. 8-13 *with* Psalm 46
Genesis 22. 1-18 *with* Psalm 16
Exodus 14. 10-31; 15. 20-21 *leading into Canticle*: Exodus 15. 1b-6, 11-13, 17, 18
Isaiah 55. 1-11 *with* Canticle: Isaiah 12. 2-6

Advent 2024 - Kingdom 2025

Services other than the Eucharist.	Purple can be used until Easter Day.	
THIRD SERVICE	**SECOND SERVICE**	**Notes**
Psalm 42; 43 Exodus 11 Ephesians 2. 11-18	Psalm 39 Leviticus 16. 2-24 Luke 23. 1-25	1984 BCP page 109.

Black can be used today.	Purple can be used until Easter Day.	
THIRD SERVICE	**SECOND SERVICE**	**Notes**
Psalm 69 Lamentations 5. 15-22 A part of **John 18.1 – 19.42** *if not used at the Principal Service* *or* Hebrews 10. 1-10	Psalm 130; 143 Genesis 22. 1-18 A part of **John 18.1 – 19.42** *if not used at the Principal Service especially in the evening* *or* John 19. 38-42 *or* Colossians 1. 18-23	1984 BCP page 112.

Purple can be used until Easter Day.		
THIRD SERVICE	**SECOND SERVICE**	**Notes**
Psalm 116 Job 19. 21-27 1 John 5. 5-12	Psalm 142 Hosea 6. 1-6 John 2. 18-22	1984 BCP page 118.

EASTER VIGIL *continued*.

Baruch 3. 9-15, 32 – 4.4 *or* Proverbs 8. 1-8, 19-21; 9. 4b-6 *with* Psalm 19
Ezekiel 36. 24-28 *with* Psalm 42; 43
Ezekiel 37. 1-14 *with* Psalm 143
Zephaniah 3. 14-20 *with* Psalm 98
Romans 6. 3-11 *with* Psalm 114
and Year A - Matthew 28. 1-10; Year B - Mark 16. 1-8; **Year C - Luke 24. 1-12**

EASTER DAY

DATE	COLLECT & PC	PRINCIPAL SERVICE
Sunday 20 April (†)	60 & 61	Acts 10. 34-43 *or* Isaiah 65. 17-25 Psalm 118. [1, 2,] 14-24 1 Corinthians 15. 19-26 *or* Acts 10. 34-43 John 20. 1-18 *or* Luke 24. 1-12
OLD TESTAMENT READINGS FOR SUNDAYS IN EASTERTIDE If the Old Testament reading is used at the Principal Service in Eastertide, the reading from Acts must be used as the New Testament reading.		

Monday in Easter Week 21 April (†)	Tuesday in Easter Week 22 April	Wednesday in Easter Week 23 April (†)
DAILY EUCHARIST		
Collect & PC 60 & 61 Acts 2. 14, 22-32 Psalm 16. 1, 5-11 Matthew 28. 8-15	Collect & PC 60 & 61 Acts 2. 14, 36-41 Psalm 33. 1-5, 18-22 John 20. 11-18	Collect & PC 60 & 61 Acts 3. 1-10 Psalm 105. 1-9 Luke 24. 13-35
Morning Prayer		
Psalm 111; [117; 146] Song of Solomon 1.9 – 2.7 Mark 16. 1-8	Psalm 112; [147. 1-12] Song of Solomon 2. 8-end Luke 24. 1-12	Psalm 113; [147. 13-end] Song of Solomon 3 Matthew 28. 16-end
Evening Prayer		
Psalm 135 Exodus 12. 1-14 1 Corinthians 15. 1-11	Psalm 136 Exodus 12. 14-36 1 Corinthians 15. 12-19	Psalm 105 Exodus 12. 37-end 1 Corinthians 15. 20-28

Advent 2024 - Kingdom 2025

THIRD SERVICE	SECOND SERVICE	Notes
Psalm 114; 117 Ezekiel 47. 1-12 John 2. 13-22	Psalm 66; 114; 117 Isaiah 43. 1-21 1 Corinthians 15. 1-11 *or* John 20. 19-23	1984 BCP page 121. Easter Week: Collect 62. (†) For weekday commemorations see page 131 & 132

Thursday in Easter Week 24 April	Mark, Evangelist moved to Monday 28 April Friday in Easter Week 25 April	Saturday in Easter Week 26 April
DAILY EUCHARIST		
Collect & PC 60 & 61 Acts 3. 11-26 Psalm 8 *or* 114 Luke 24. 36b-48	Collect & PC 60 & 61 Acts 4. 1-12 Psalm 116. 1-9 John 21. 1-14	Collect & PC 60 & 61 Acts 4. 13-21 Psalm 118. 1-4, 22-29 Mark 16. 9-15
Morning Prayer		
Psalm 114; [148] Song of Solomon 5.2 – 6.3 Luke 7. 11-17	Psalm 115; [149] Song of Solomon 7.10 – 8.4 Luke 8. 41-end	Psalm 116; [150] Song of Solomon 8. 5-7 John 11. 17-44
Evening Prayer		
Psalm 106 Exodus 13. 1-16 1 Corinthians 15. 29-34	Psalm 107 Exodus 13.17 – 14.14 1 Corinthians 15. 35-50	Psalm 145 Exodus 14. 15-end 1 Corinthians 15. 51-end

Year C - Weekdays 1

THE SECOND SUNDAY of EASTER

DATE	COLLECT & PC	PRINCIPAL SERVICE	
Sunday 27 April	63 & 64	*Either:* Acts 5. 27-32 Psalm 118. 14-29; *or* 150 Revelation 1. 4-8 John 20. 19-31	*or (with OT reading):* Exodus 14. 10-31; 15. 20, 21 Psalm 118. 14-29 or 150 Acts 5. 27-32 John 20. 19-31

* Mark, Evangelist *(moved from 25 April)* **Monday 28 April**	† Catherine of Siena **Tuesday 29 April**	**Wednesday 30 April**
	DAILY EUCHARIST	
Collect & PC 188 & 127 Proverbs 15. 28-33 *or* Acts 15. 35-41 Psalm 119. 9-16 Ephesians 4. 7-16 Mark 13. 5-13	Collect & PC 63 & 64 Acts 4. 32-37 Psalm 93 John 3. 7-15	Collect & PC 63 & 64 Acts 5. 17-26 Psalm 34. 1-8 John 3. 16-21
	Morning Prayer	
Psalm 37. 23-40 Isaiah 62. 6-10 *or* Sirach 51. 13-30 Acts 12.25 – 13.13	Psalm 8; [20; 21] Deuteronomy 1. 19-40 John 20. 11-18	Psalm [16;] 30 Deuteronomy 3. 18-end John 20. 19-end
	Evening Prayer	
Psalm 45 Ezekiel 1. 4-14 2 Timothy 4. 1-11	Psalm 104 Exodus 15.22 – 16.10 Colossians 1. 15-end	Psalm 33 Exodus 16. 11-end Colossians 2. 1-15
		... eve of Philip and James: Psalm 25: Isaiah 40. 27-31: John 12. 20-26

Advent 2024 - Kingdom 2025

THIRD SERVICE	SECOND SERVICE	Notes
Psalm 136. 1-16 Exodus 12. 1-13 1 Peter 1. 3-12	Psalm 16 Isaiah 52.13 – 53.12 *or* 53. 1-6, 9-12 Luke 24. 13-35	1984 BCP page 129. * For the replaced readings, see page 116. † For weekday commemorations see page 131 & 132.

Evening Prayer on the eve of the Mark: Psalm 19; Isaiah 52. 7-10; Mark 1. 1-15

THANKSGIVING FOR HOLY BAPTISM
The readings may be used at the Eucharist or a non-Eucharistic service and can be celebrated at any time during Eastertide. See page 155.

* Philip *and* James, Apostles **Thursday 1 May**	† Athanasius **Friday 2 May**	† Henry Vaughan **Saturday 3 May**
DAILY EUCHARIST		
Collect & PC 190 & 110 Isaiah 30. 15-21 Psalm 119. 1-8 Ephesians 1. 3-10 John 14. 1-14	Collect & PC 63 & 64 Acts 5. 34-42 Psalm 27. 1-6, 13, 14 John 6. 1-15	Collect & PC 63 & 64 Acts 6. 1-7 Psalm 33. 1-5, 18-22 John 6. 16-21
Morning Prayer		
Psalm 139 Proverbs 4. 10-18 James 1. 1-12	Psalm [57;] 61 Deuteronomy 4. 15-31 John 21. 15-19	Psalm [63;] 84 Deuteronomy 4. 32-40 John 21. 20-end
Evening Prayer		
Psalm 149 Job 23. 1-12 John 1. 43-51	Psalm 118 Exodus 18. 1-12 Colossians 3.12 – 4.1	Psalm 66 Exodus 18. 13-end Colossians 4. 2-end

THE THIRD SUNDAY *of* EASTER

DATE	COLLECT & PC	PRINCIPAL SERVICE	
Sunday 4 May	65 & 66	*Either:* Acts 9. 1-6, [7-20] Psalm 30 Revelation 5. 11-14 John 21. 1-19	*or (with OT reading):* Zephaniah 3. 14-20 Psalm 30 Acts 9. 1-6, [7-20] John 21. 1-19

† Asaph

Monday 5 May	Tuesday 6 May	Wednesday 7 May
DAILY EUCHARIST		
Collect & PC 65 & 66 Acts 6. 8-15 Psalm 119. 161-168 John 6. 22-29	Collect & PC 65 & 66 Acts 7. 51 – 8.1a Psalm 31. 1-5 John 6. 30-35	Collect & PC 65 & 66 Acts 8. 1b-8 Psalm 66. 1-7 John 6. 35-40
Morning Prayer		
Psalm 96; [97] Deuteronomy 5. 1-22 Ephesians 1. 1-14	Psalm 98; [99; 100] Deuteronomy 5. 22-end Ephesians 1. 15-end	Psalm 105 Deuteronomy 6 Ephesians 2. 1-10
Evening Prayer		
Psalm 61; [65] Exodus 19 Luke 1. 1-25	Psalm 71 Exodus 20. 1-21 Luke 1. 26-38	Psalm [67;] 72 Exodus 24 Luke 1. 39-56

THIRD SERVICE	SECOND SERVICE	Notes
Psalm 80. 1-7 Exodus 15. 1, 2, 9-18 John 10. 1-19	Psalm 86 Isaiah 38. 9-20 John 11. [17-26,] 27-44	1984 BCP page 132. Thanksgiving for Holy Baptism, see page 155. † For weekday commemorations see page 133.

	† Julian of Norwich	† Gregory of Nazianzus	
	Thursday 8 May	Friday 9 May	Saturday 10 May
		DAILY EUCHARIST	
	Collect & PC 65 & 66 Acts 8. 26-40 Psalm 66. 8, 9, 16-20 John 6. 44-51	Collect & PC 65 & 66 Acts 9. 1-20 Psalm 117 John 6. 52-59	Collect & PC 65 & 66 Acts 9. 31-42 Psalm 116. 12-19 John 6. 60-69
		Morning Prayer	
	Psalm 136 Deuteronomy 7. 1-11 Ephesians 2. 11-end	Psalm 107 Deuteronomy 7. 12-end Ephesians 3. 1-13	Psalm [108;] 110; [111] Deuteronomy 8 Ephesians 3. 14-end
		Evening Prayer	
	Psalm 73 Exodus 25. 1-22 Luke 1. 57-end	Psalm 77 Exodus 28. 1-4a, 29-38 Luke 2. 1-20	Psalm [23;] 27 Exodus 29. 1-9 Luke 2. 21-40

Year C - Weekdays 1

THE FOURTH SUNDAY of EASTER

DATE	COLLECT & PC	PRINCIPAL SERVICE	
Sunday 11 May Christian Aid week	67 & 68	*Either:* Acts 9. 36-43 Psalm 23 Revelation 7. 9-17 John 10. 22-30	or (with OT reading): Genesis 7. 1-5, 11-18; 8. 6-18; 9. 8-13 Psalm 23 Acts 9. 36-43 John 10. 22-30

Monday 12 May	Tuesday 13 May	* Matthias, Apostle Wednesday 14 May
DAILY EUCHARIST		
Collect & PC 67 & 68 Acts 11. 1-18 Psalm 43 John 10. 1-10	Collect & PC 67 & 68 Acts 11. 19-26 Psalm 87 John 10. 22-30	**Collect & PC 196 & 110 Isaiah 22. 15-25 Psalm 15 Acts 1. 15-26 John 15. 9-17 or Acts 1. 15-26 Psalm 15 1 Corinthians 4. 1-7 John 15. 9-17**
Morning Prayer		
Psalm 103 Deuteronomy 9. 1-21 Ephesians 4. 1-16	Psalm 139 Deuteronomy 9.23 – 10.5 Ephesians 4. 17-end	Psalm 16 1 Samuel 2. 27-35 Acts 2. 37-47
Evening Prayer		
Psalm [112; 113;] 114 Exodus 32. 1-14 Luke 2. 41-end	Psalm [115;] 116 Exodus 32. 15-34 Luke 3. 1-14 ... *eve of Matthias:*	Psalm 80 1 Samuel 16. 1-13a Matthew 7. 15-27
Psalm 147: Isaiah 22. 15-22: Philippians 3.13b – 4.1		

THIRD SERVICE	SECOND SERVICE	Notes
Psalm 146 1 Kings 17. 17-24 Luke 7. 11-23	Psalm 113; 114 Isaiah 63. 7-14 Luke 24. 36-49	1984 BCP page 134. Thanksgiving for Holy Baptism, see page 155. * For the replaced readings, see page 116. † For weekday commemorations see page 133.

† Edmwnd Prys *and* John Davies

Thursday 15 May	Friday 16 May	Saturday 17 May
DAILY EUCHARIST		
Collect & PC 67 & 68 Acts 13. 13-25 Psalm 89. 1, 2, 19-26 John 13. 16-20	Collect & PC 67 & 68 Acts 13. 26-33 Psalm 2 John 14. 1-7	Collect & PC 67 & 68 Acts 13. 44-52 Psalm 98 John 14. 7-14
Morning Prayer		
Psalm 118 Deuteronomy 11. 8-end Ephesians 5. 15-end	Psalm 33 Deuteronomy 12. 1-14 Ephesians 6. 1-9	Psalm 34 Deuteronomy 15. 1-18 Ephesians 6. 10-end
Evening Prayer		
Psalm [81;] 85 Exodus 34. 1-10, 27-end Luke 4. 1-13	Psalm 36; [40] Exodus 35.20 – 36.7 Luke 4. 14-30	Psalm 84; [86] Exodus 40. 17-end Luke 4. 31-37

THE FIFTH SUNDAY of EASTER

DATE	COLLECT & PC	PRINCIPAL SERVICE	
Sunday 18 May	69 & 70	*Either:* Acts 11. 1-18 Psalm 148 *or* 148. 1-6 Revelation 21. 1-6 John 13. 31-35	*or (with OT reading):* Baruch 3. 9-15, 32 – 4.4 *or* Genesis 22. 1-18 Psalm 148 *or* 148. 1-6 Acts 11. 1-18 John 13. 31-35

† Dunstan		
Monday 19 May	Tuesday 20 May	Wednesday 21 May
DAILY EUCHARIST		
Collect & PC 69 & 70 Acts 14. 5-18 Psalm 115. 1-12a John 14. 21-26	Collect & PC 69 & 70 Acts 14. 19-27 Psalm 145. 10-13, 22 John 14. 27-31a	Collect & PC 69 & 70 Acts 15. 1-6 Psalm 122 John 15. 1-8
Morning Prayer		
Psalm 145 Deuteronomy 16. 1-20 1 Peter 1. 1-12	Psalm 19; [147.1-12] Deuteronomy 17. 8-end 1 Peter 1. 13-end	Psalm 30; [147. 13-end] Deuteronomy 18. 9-end 1 Peter 2. 1-10
Evening Prayer		
Psalm 105 Numbers 9. 15-end; 10. 33-end Luke 4. 38-end	Psalm [96;] 97 Numbers 11. 1-33 Luke 5. 1-11	Psalm [98;] 99; [100] Numbers 12 Luke 5. 12-26

THIRD SERVICE	SECOND SERVICE	Notes
Psalm 16 2 Samuel 7. 4-13 Acts 2. 14a, 22-32, [33-36]	Psalm 98 Daniel 6. [1-5,] 6-23 Mark 15.46 – 16.8	1984 BCP page 137. Thanksgiving for Holy Baptism, see page 155. † For weekday commemorations see page 133 & 134.

		† Charles Wesley *and* John Wesley
Thursday 22 May	Friday 23 May	Saturday 24 May
DAILY EUCHARIST		
Collect & PC 69 & 70 Acts 15. 7-21 Psalm 96. 1-3, 10-13 John 15. 9-11	Collect & PC 69 & 70 Acts 15. 22-31 Psalm 57. 5-11 John 15. 12-17	Collect & PC 69 & 70 Acts 16. 1-10 Psalm 100 John 15.18-21
Morning Prayer		
Psalm 57; [148] Deuteronomy 19 1 Peter 2. 11-end	Psalm 138; [149] Deuteronomy 21.22 – 22.8 1 Peter 3. 1-12	Psalm 146; [150] Deuteronomy 24. 5-end 1 Peter 3. 13-end
Evening Prayer		
Psalm 104 Numbers 13. 1-3, 17-end Luke 5. 27-end	Psalm 66 Numbers 14. 1-25 Luke 6. 1-11	Psalm 118 Numbers 14. 26-end Luke 6. 12-26

THE SIXTH SUNDAY *of* EASTER: ROGATION SUNDAY

DATE	COLLECT & PC	PRINCIPAL SERVICE	
Sunday 25 May (†)	71 & 72	*Either:* Acts 16. 9-15 Psalm 67 Revelation 21. 10, 22 – 22.5	*or (with OT reading):* Ezekiel 37. 1-14 Psalm 67 Acts 16. 9-15
Anglican Communion Sunday		John 14. 23-29 *or* John 5. 1-9	John 14. 23-29 *or* John 5. 1-9

Rogation Day (†) Monday 26 May	Rogation Day Tuesday 27 May	Rogation Day (†) Wednesday 28 May
DAILY EUCHARIST		
Collect & PC 341 & 344 1 Kings 8. 35-40 Psalm 104. 19-30 1 John 5. 12-15 Matthew 6. 1-15	Collect & PC 342 & 344 Job 28. 1-11 Psalm 107. 1-9 2 Thessalonians 3. 6-13 Mark 11. 22-24	Collect & PC 343 & 344 Deuteronomy 8. 1-10 Psalm 121 Philippians 4. 4-7 Luke 11. 5-13
Morning Prayer		
Psalm 65; [67] Deuteronomy 26 1 Peter 4. 1-11	Ps. [124; 125;] 126; [127] Deuteronomy 28. 1-14 1 Peter 4. 12-end	Psalm 132; [133] Deuteronomy 28. 58-end 1 Peter 5
Evening Prayer *… on the eve of Ascension Day:*		
Psalm 121; [122; 123] Numbers 16. 1-35 Luke 6. 27-38	Ps. 128; [129; 130; 131] Numbers 16. 36-end Luke 6. 39-end	Psalms 15; 24 2 Samuel 23. 1-5 Colossians 2.20 – 3.4

Advent 2024 - Kingdom 2025

THIRD SERVICE	SECOND SERVICE	Notes
Psalm 40. 1-8	Psalm 126; 127	1984 BCP page 140.
Genesis 1. 26-28, [29-31]	Zephaniah 3. 14-20	(†) For weekday commemorations see page 134.
Colossians 3. 1-11	Matthew 28. 1-10, 16-20	
	Thanksgiving for Holy Baptism, see page 155.	* For the replaced readings, see page 116.

ASCENSION DAY **The reading from Acts must be used as either the first or second reading.*	Prayers for the gifts of the Holy Spirit begins. (between Ascension Day and Pentecost)	
		* The Visit of the Virgin Mary to Elizabeth
Thursday 29 May	Friday 30 May	Saturday 31 May
PRINCIPAL SERVICE	**DAILY EUCHARIST**	
Collect & PC 73 & 74	Collect & PC 71 & 72	Collect & PC 204 & 8
** Acts 1. 1-11 *or* Daniel 7. 9-14	Acts 18. 9-18	Zephaniah 3. 14-18
Psalm 47 *or* 93	Psalm 47. 1-5	Psalm 113
Ephesians 1. 15-23 *or* ** Acts 1. 1-11	John 16. 20-24	Romans 12. 9-16
Luke 24. 44-53		Luke 1. 39-49, [50-56]
THIRD SERVICE	**Morning Prayer**	
Psalm 110	Psalm [20,] 81	Psalm 85
Isaiah 52. 7-15	Deuteronomy 29. 2-15	1 Samuel 2. 1-10
Hebrews 7. [11-25,] 26-28	1 John 1.1 – 2.6	Mark 3. 31-35
SECOND SERVICE	**Evening Prayer**	
Psalm 8	Psalm 145	Psalm 122; 127; 128
Song of the Three 29-37 *or* 2 Kings 2. 1-15	Numbers 20. 1-13	Zechariah 2. 10-13
Revelation 5	Luke 7. 11-17	John 3. 25-30
If the Second Service is a Eucharist, the Gospel is: Matthew 28. 16-20	*... eve of the Visit:* Psalm 45: Song of Solomon 2. 8-14: Luke 1. 26-38	

Year C - Weekdays 1

THE SEVENTH SUNDAY *of* EASTER - Sunday after Ascension Day

DATE	COLLECT & PC	PRINCIPAL SERVICE	
Sunday 1 June (†)	75 & 76	*Either:* Acts 16. 16-34 Psalm 97 Revelation 22. 12-14, 16, 17, 20, 21 John 17. 20-26	*or (with OT reading):* Ezekiel 36. 24-28 Psalm 97 Acts 16. 16-34 John 17. 20-26
Ministry and Calling Sunday			

Prayers for the gifts of the Holy Spirit *continues* (between Ascension Day and Pentecost).

† Blandina *and* her Companions	† James Hannington, The Martyrs of Uganda *and* Janani Luwum	
Monday 2 June	Tuesday 3 June	Wednesday 4 June
DAILY EUCHARIST		
Collect & PC 75 & 76 Acts 19. 1-10 Psalm 68. 1-6 John 16. 29-33	Collect & PC 75 & 76 Acts 20. 17-27 Psalm 68. 7-20 John 17. 1-11a	Collect & PC 75 & 76 Acts 20. 28-38 Psalm 68. 28-35 John 17. 11b-19
Morning Prayer		
Psalm 93; [96; 97] Deuteronomy 31. 1-13 1 John 2. 18-end	Psalm [98; 99;] 100 Deuteronomy 31. 14-29 1 John 3. 1-10	Psalm [2;] 29 Deuteron. 31.30 – 32.14 1 John 3. 11-end
Evening Prayer		
Psalm 18 Numbers 22. 1-35 Luke 7. 36-end	Psalm 68 Numbers 22.36 – 23.12 Luke 8. 1-15	Psalm [36;] 46 Numbers 23. 13-end Luke 8. 16-25

Advent 2024 - Kingdom 2025

THIRD SERVICE	SECOND SERVICE	Notes
Psalm 99 Deuteronomy 34 Luke 24. 44-53 or Acts 1. 1-8	Psalm 68 or 68. 1-14, 19, 20 Isaiah 44. 1-8 Ephesians 4. 7-16 *If the Second Service is a Eucharist, the Gospel is:* Luke 24. 44-53	1984 BCP page 145. Thanksgiving for Holy Baptism, see page 155. † For weekday commemorations see page 135.

Prayers for the gifts of the Holy Spirit *continues*

World Environment Day
† Boniface

Thursday 5 June	Friday 6 June	Saturday 7 June
DAILY EUCHARIST		
Collect & PC 75 & 76 Acts 22. 30; 23. 6-11 Psalm 16 John 17. 20-26	Collect & PC 75 & 76 Acts 25. 13-21 Psalm 103. 1, 2, 19-22 John 21. 15-19	Collect & PC 75 & 76 Acts 28. 16-20, 30, 31 Psalm 11 John 21. 20-25
Morning Prayer		
Psalm 24; [72] Deuteronomy 32. 15-47 1 John 4. 1-6	Psalm 28; [30] Deuteronomy 33 1 John 4. 7-end	Psalm [42;] 43 Deuteron. 32. 48-end; 34 1 John 5
Evening Prayer ... *on th eve of the Day of Pentecost*		
Psalm 139 Numbers 24 Luke 8. 26-39	Psalm 147 Numbers 27. 12-end Luke 8. 40-end	Psalm 48 Deuteronomy 16. 9-15 John 7. 37-39

Year C - Weekdays 1

THE DAY *of* PENTECOST - Whitsunday

DATE	COLLECT & PC	PRINCIPAL SERVICE
Sunday 8 June	77 & 78	*The reading from Acts must be used as either the first or second reading.* Acts 2. 1-21 *or* Genesis 11. 1-9 Psalm 104. 24-34, 35b *or* 104. 24-36 Romans 8. 14-17 *or* Acts 2. 1-21 John 14. 8-17, [25-27]

† Columba Monday 9 June	† Ephrem of Syria Tuesday 10 June	* Barnabas, Apostle Wednesday 11 June
DAILY EUCHARIST		
Collect & PC 79 & 80 2 Corinthians 1.1-7 Psalm 34. 1-8 Matthew 5. 1-12	Collect & PC 79 & 80 2 Corinthians 1. 18-22 Psalm 119. 129-136 Matthew 5. 13-16	Collect & PC 211 & 110 Job 29. 11-16 Psalm 112 Acts 11. 19-30 John 15. 12-17 *or* Acts 11. 19-30 Psalm 112 Galatians 2. 1-10 John 15. 12-17
Morning Prayer		
Psalm [123; 124; 125;] 126 Job 1 Romans 1. 1-17	Psalm 132; [133] Job 2 Romans 1. 18-end	Psalm 100; 101 Jeremiah 9. 23, 24 Acts 4. 32-37
Evening Prayer		
Psalm 127; [128; 129] Joshua 1 Luke 9. 18-27	Psalm [134;] 135 Joshua 2 Luke 9. 28-36	Psalm 147 Ecclesiastes 12. 9-14 *or* Tobit 4. 5-11 Acts 9. 26-31

... eve of Barnabas:
Psalm 1; 15: Isaiah 42. 5-12: Acts 14. 8-28

Advent 2024 - Kingdom 2025

THIRD SERVICE	SECOND SERVICE	Notes
Psalm 33. 1-12 Isaiah 40. 12-23 *or* Wisdom 9. 9-17 1 Corinthians 2. 6-16	Psalm 36. 5-10; 150 Exodus 33. 7-20 2 Corinthians 3. 4-18 *If the Second Service is a Eucharist, the Gospel is:* John 16. 4b-15	1984 BCP page 147. The weekdays after the Day of Pentecost, use Collect 77. * For the replaced readings, see page 116. † For weekday commemorations see page 135 & 136.

		Basil the Great
Thursday 12 June	Friday 13 June	Saturday 14 June
DAILY EUCHARIST		
Collect & PC 79 & 80 2 Corinthians 3.12 – 4.6 Psalm 85. 7-13 Matthew 5. 20-26	Collect & PC 79 & 80 2 Corinthians 4. 7-15 Psalm 116. 9-17 Matthew 5. 27-32	Collect & PC 79 & 80 2 Corinthians 5. 14-21 Psalm 103. 1-12 Matthew 5. 33-37
Morning Prayer		
Psalm 14 Job 4 Romans 2. 17-end	Psalm [142;] 144 Job 5 Romans 3. 1-20	Psalm 147 Job 6 Romans 3. 21-end
Evening Prayer		
Psalm 138; [140; 141] Joshua 4.1 – 5.1 Luke 9. 51-end	Psalm 145 Joshua 5. 2-end Luke 10. 1-16	Psalm 148; [149; 150] Joshua 6. 1-20 Luke 10. 17-24
		… on the eve of Trinity Sunday: *Psalm 97; 98: Isaiah 40. 12-31: Mark 1. 1-13*

Year C - Weekdays 1

TRINITY SUNDAY		
DATE	**COLLECT & PC**	**PRINCIPAL SERVICE**
Sunday 15 June	81 & 82	Proverbs 8. 1-4, 22-31 Psalm 8 Romans 5. 1-5 John 16. 12-15

† Richard

Monday 16 June	Tuesday 17 June	Wednesday 18 June
DAILY EUCHARIST		
Collect & PC 81 & 82 2 Corinthians 6. 1-10 Psalm 98 Matthew 5. 38-42	Collect & PC 81 & 82 2 Corinthians 8. 1-9 Psalm 146 Matthew 5. 43-48	Collect & PC 81 & 82 2 Corinthians 9. 6-11 Psalm 112. 1-9 Matthew 6. 1-6. 16-18
Morning Prayer		
Psalm 1; [2; 3] Job 7 Romans 4. 1-12	Psalm 5; [6; 8] Job 8 Romans 4. 13-end	Psalm 119. 1-32 Job 9 Romans 5. 1-11
Evening Prayer		
Psalm 4; [7] Joshua 7. 1-15 Luke 10. 25-37	Psalm 9; [10] Joshua 7. 16-end Luke 10. 38-end	Psalm 11; [12; 13] Joshua 8. 1-29 Luke 11. 1-13

... eve of the Thanksgiving:
Psalm 110; 111: Exodus 16. 2-15: John 6. 22-35

Advent 2024 - Kingdom 2025

THIRD SERVICE	SECOND SERVICE	Notes
Psalm 29 Isaiah 6. 1-8, [9, 10] Revelation 4	Psalm 73. 1-3, 16-28 Exodus 3. 1-15 John 3. 1-17	1984 BCP page 154. * For the replaced readings, see page 117. † For weekday commemorations see page 136.

* Thanksgiving for Holy Communion (Corpus Christi) Thursday 19 June	World Refugee Day † Alban, Julius *and* Aaron Friday 20 June	Saturday 21 June
	DAILY EUCHARIST	
Collect & PC 339 & 55 Genesis 14. 18-20 Psalm 116. 12-19 1 Corinthians 11. 23-26, [27-29, 31-34a] John 6. [47-50,] 51-58	Collect & PC 81 & 82 2 Corinth. 11. 18, 21b-30 Psalm 34 1-6 Matthew 6. 19-23	Collect & PC 81 & 82 2 Corinthians 12. 1-10 Psalm 34. 7-14 Matthew 6. 24-34
	Morning Prayer	
Psalm 147 Deuteronomy 8. 2-16 1 Corinthians 10. 1-17	Psalm [17;] 19 Job 11 Romans 6. 1-14	Psalm [20; 21;] 23 Job 12 Romans 6. 15-end
	Evening Prayer	
Psalm 23; 42; 43 Proverbs 9. 1-5 Luke 9. 11-17	Psalm 22 Joshua 9. 3-26 Luke 11. 29-36	Psalm 24; [25] Joshua 10. 1-15 Luke 11. 37-end

Year C - Weekdays 1

THE FIRST SUNDAY *after* TRINITY (Proper 7)

DATE	COLLECT & PC	PRINCIPAL SERVICE	
Sunday 22 June	83 & 84	*Continuous:* 1 Kings 19. 1-4, [5-7,] 8-15a Psalm 42 *and / or* 43 Galatians 3. 23-29 Luke 8. 26-39	*or Related:* Isaiah 65. 1-9 Psalm 22. 19-28 Galatians 3. 23-29 Luke 8. 26-39
Covenant Sunday			

Monday 23 June	* The Nativity of John the Baptist Tuesday 24 June	Ember Day Wednesday 25 June
DAILY EUCHARIST		
Collect & PC 83 & 84 Genesis 12. 1-9 Psalm 33. 12-22 Matthew 7. 1-5	Collect & PC 215 & 5 Isaiah 40. 1-11 Psalm 85. 5-12 Acts 13. 14b-2 *or* Galatians 3. 23-29 Luke 1. 57-66, 8	Collect & PC 351 & 352 Ember set 1, 2 *or* 3 See page 154.
Morning Prayer		
Psalm [27;] 30 Job 13 Romans 7. 1-6	Psalm 50 Sirach 48. 1-10 *or* Malachi 3. 1-6 Luke 3. 1-17	Psalm 34 Job 15 Romans 8. 1-11
Evening Prayer		
Psalm [26;] 28; [29] Joshua 14 Luke 12. 1-12	Psalm 80; 82 Malachi 4 Matthew 11. 2-19	Psalm 119. 33-56 Joshua 22. 9-end Luke 12. 22-31
... eve of John the Baptist: *Psalm 71: Judges 13. 2-7, 24, 25: Luke 1. 5-25*		

Advent 2024 - Kingdom 2025

THIRD SERVICE	SECOND SERVICE	Notes
Psalm 55. 1-14, 16-19 Deuteronomy 11. 1-15 Acts 27. 1-12	Psalm [50;] 57 Genesis 24. 1-27 Mark 5. 21-43	1984 BCP page 157 * For the replaced readings, see page 117. † For weekday commemorations see page 136.

	† Irenæus	
	Ember Day	Ember Day
Thursday 26 June	Friday 27 June	Saturday 28 June
DAILY EUCHARIST		
Collect & PC 83 & 84 Genesis 16. 1-12, 15, 16 Psalm 106 1-5 Matthew 7. 21-29	Collect & PC 351 & 352 Ember set 1,2 *or* 3 See page 154.	Collect & PC 351 & 352 Ember set 1, 2 *or* 3 See page 154.
Morning Prayer		
Psalm 37 Job 16.1 – 17.2 Romans 8. 12-17	Psalm 31 Job 17. 3-end Romans 8. 18-30	Psalm [41;] 42; [43] Job 18 Romans 8. 31-end
Evening Prayer		
Psalm [39;] 40 Joshua 23 Luke 12. 32-40	Psalm 35 Joshua 24. 1-28 Luke 12. 41-48	Psalm [45;] 46 Joshua 24. 29-end Luke 12. 49-end

... eve of Peter or Peter and Paul:
For a full list of Readings see page 136

Year C - Weekdays 1

PETER, APOSTLE *or* PETER AND PAUL, APOSTLES		
DATE	COLLECT & PC	PRINCIPAL SERVICE
Sunday 29 June	Peter: 217 & 110 Peter and Paul 218 & 110	Peter *or* Peter and Paul: *For a full list of Readings at the Eucharist see page 137.*

† The Martyrdom of Paul	† Euddogwy	
Monday 30 June	**Tuesday 1 July**	**Wednesday 2 July**
DAILY EUCHARIST		
Collect & PC 85 & 86 Genesis 18. 16-33 Psalm 103. 1-10 Matthew 8. 18-22	Collect & PC 85 & 86 Genesis 19. 15-29 Psalm 26 Matthew 8. 23-27	Collect & PC 85 & 86 Genesis 21. 5, 8-20 Psalm 34. 1-8 Matthew 8. 28-34
Morning Prayer		
Psalm 44 Job 19 Romans 9. 1-18	Psalm 48; [52] Job 21 Romans 9. 19-end	Psalm 119. 57-80 Job 22 Romans 10. 1-10
Evening Prayer		
Psalm 47; [49] Judges 2 Luke 13 .1-9	Psalm 50 Judges 4. 1-23 Luke 13. 10-21	Psalm 59; [60; 67] Judges 5 Luke 13. 22-end
		... on the eve of Thomas: Psalm 27: Isaiah 35: Hebrews 10.35 – 11.1

Advent 2024 - Kingdom 2025

THIRD SERVICE	SECOND SERVICE	Notes
Psalm 71 Isaiah 49. 1-6 Acts 11. 1-18	Psalm 124; 138 Ezekiel 34. 11-16 John 21. 15-22	1984 BCP page 255. * For the replaced readings, see page 117. † For weekday commemorations see page 137 & 138.

* Thomas, Apostle Thursday 3 July	† Peblig Friday 4 July	Saturday 5 July
DAILY EUCHARIST		
Collect & PC 221 & 110 Habakkuk 2. 1-4 Psalm 31. 1-5 Ephesians 2. 19-22 John 20. 24-29, [30, 31]	Collect & PC 85 & 86 Genesis 23. 1-4, 19; 24. 1-8, 62-67 Psalm 106 1-5 Matthew 9. 9-13	Collect & PC 85 & 86 Genesis 27. 1-9, 15-29 Psalm 135. 1-6 Matthew 9. 14-17
Morning Prayer		
Psalm 92; 146 2 Samuel 15. 17-21 *or* Sirach 2 John 11. 1-16	Psalm 51; [54] Job 24 Romans 11. 1-12	Psalm 68 Job 25 – *end of* 26 Romans 11. 13-24
Evening Prayer		
Psalm 139 Job 42. 1-6 1 Peter 1. 3-12	Psalm 38 Judges 6. 25-end Luke 14. 12-24	Psalm [65;] 66 Judges 7 Luke 14. 25-end

Year C - Weekdays 1

THE THIRD SUNDAY *after* TRINITY (Proper 9)

DATE	COLLECT & PC	PRINCIPAL SERVICE	
Sunday 6 July (†)	87 & 88	*Continuous:* 2 Kings 5. 1-14 Psalm 30 Galatians 6. [1-6,] 7-16 Luke 10. 1-11, 16-20	*or Related:* Isaiah 66. 10-14 Psalm 66. 1-9 Galatians 6. [1-6,] 7-16 Luke 10. 1-11, 16-20

Monday 7 July	Tuesday 8 July	Wednesday 9 July
DAILY EUCHARIST		
Collect & PC 87 & 88 Genesis 28. 10-22 Psalm 91. 1-6, 14-16 Matthew 9. 18-26	Collect & PC 87 & 88 Genesis 32. 22-32 Psalm 17. 1-8 Matthew 9. 32-38	Collect & PC 87 & 88 Genesis 41. 55-57; 42. 5-7a, 17-24a Psalm 33. 1-5, 18-22 Matthew 10. 1-7
Morning Prayer		
Psalm 71 Job 27 Romans 11. 25-end	Psalm 73 Job 28 Romans 12. 1-8	Psalm 77 Job 29 Romans 12. 9-end
Evening Prayer		
Psalm 72; [75] Judges 8. 22-end Luke 15. 1-10	Psalm 74 Judges 9. 1-21 Luke 15. 11-end	Psalm 119. 81-104 Judges 9. 22-end Luke 16. 1-18

Advent 2024 - Kingdom 2025

THIRD SERVICE	SECOND SERVICE	Notes
Psalm 74 Deuteronomy 24. 10-22 Acts 28. 1-16	Psalm 65; [70] Genesis 29. 1-20 Mark 6. 7-29	1984 BCP page 162. † For weekday commemorations see page 138.

† Benedict of Nursia

Thursday 10 July	Friday 11 July	Saturday 12 July
DAILY EUCHARIST		
Collect & PC 87 & 88 Genesis 44.18 – 45.5 Psalm 105. 7-22 Matthew 10. 7-15	Collect & PC 87 & 88 Genesis 46. 1-7, 28-30 Psalm 37. 3-6, 18-24 Matthew 10. 16-23	Collect & PC 87 & 88 Genesis 49. 29-33 Psalm 105. 1-7 Matthew 10. 24-33
Morning Prayer		
Psalm 78. 1-39 Job 30 Romans 13. 1-7	Psalm 55 Job 31 Romans 13. 8-end	Psalm 76; [79] Job 32 Romans 14. 1-12
Evening Prayer		
Psalm 78. 40-end Judges 11. 1-11 Luke 16. 19-end	Psalm 69 Judges 11. 29-end Luke 17. 1-10	Psalm [81;] 84 Judges 12. 1-7 Luke 17. 11-19

THE FOURTH SUNDAY *after* TRINITY (Proper 10)

DATE	COLLECT & PC	PRINCIPAL SERVICE	
Sunday 13 July Sea Sunday	89 & 90	*Continuous:* Amos 7. 7-17 Psalm 82 Colossians 1. 1-14 Luke 10. 25-37	*or Related:* Deuteronomy 30. 9-14 Psalm 25. 1-10 Colossians 1. 1-14 Luke 10. 25-37

† John Keble

Monday 14 July	Tuesday 15 July	Wednesday 16 July
DAILY EUCHARIST		
Collect & PC 89 & 90 Exodus 1. 8-14, 22 Psalm 124 Matthew 10.34 – 11.1	Collect & PC 89 & 90 Exodus 2. 1-15 Psalm 69. 1, 2, 32-36 Matthew 11. 20-24	Collect & PC 89 & 90 Exodus 3. 1-12 Psalm 103. 1-7 Matthew 11. 25-27
Psalm 80; [82] Job 33 Romans 14. 13-end	Psalm [87;] 89. 1-18 Job 38 Romans 15. 1-13	Psalm 119. 105-128 Job 39 Romans 15. 14-21
Evening Prayer		
Psalm [85;] 86 Judges 13. 1-24 Luke 17. 20-end	Psalm 89.19-end Judges 14 Luke 18. 1-14	Psalm 91; [93] Judges 15.1 – 16.3 Luke 18. 15-30

Advent 2024 - Kingdom 2025

THIRD SERVICE	SECOND SERVICE	Notes
Psalm 76 Deuteronomy 28. 1-14 Acts 28. 17-31	Psalm 77 *or* 77. 1-12 Genesis 32. 9-30 Mark 7. 1-23	1984 BCP page 165. † For weekday commemorations see page 138.

	† Elizabeth of Russia	† Gregory and his sister Macrina
Thursday 17 July	**Friday 18 July**	**Saturday 19 July**
DAILY EUCHARIST		
Collect & PC 89 & 90 Exodus 3. 13-20 Psalm 105. 1-15 Matthew 11. 28-30	Collect & PC 89 & 90 Exodus 11.10 – 12.14 Psalm 116. 12-19 Matthew 12. 1-8	Collect & PC 89 & 90 Exodus 12. 37-42 Psalm 136. 1-3, 10-15 Matthew 12. 14-21
Psalm [90;] 92 Job 40 Romans 15. 22-end	Psalm 88; [95] Job 41 Romans 16. 1-16	Psalm [96;] 97; [100] Job 42 Romans 16. 17-end
Evening Prayer		
Psalm 94 Judges 16. 4-end Luke 18. 31-end	Psalm 102 Judges 17 Luke 19. 1-10	Psalm 104 Judges 18. 1-20, 27-end Luke 19. 11-27

Year C - Weekdays 1

THE FIFTH SUNDAY *after* TRINITY (Proper 11)

DATE	COLLECT & PC	PRINCIPAL SERVICE	
Sunday 20 July	91 & 92	*Continuous:* Amos 8. 1-12 Psalm 52 Colossians 1. 15-28 Luke 10. 38-42	*or Related:* Genesis 18. 1-10a Psalm 15 Colossians 1. 15-28 Luke 10. 38-42

† Howell Harris	* Mary Magdalene	† Bridget of Sweden
Monday 21 July	Tuesday 22 July	Wednesday 23 July
DAILY EUCHARIST		
Collect & PC 91 & 92 Exodus 14. 5-18 Psalm 114 Matthew 12. 38-42	Collect & PC 229 & 90 Song of Solomon 3. 1-4 Psalm 42. 1-8 2 Corinthians 5. 14-17 John 20. 1, 2, 11-18	Collect & PC 91 & 92 Exodus 16. 1-5, 9-15 Psalm 78. 18-29 Matthew 13. 1-9
Morning Prayer		
Psalm 98; [99; 101] Ezekiel 1. 1-14 2 Corinthians 1. 1-14	Psalm 63 Zephaniah 3. 14-20 Mark 15.40 – 16.7	Psalm [110;] 111; [112] Ezekiel 2.3 – 3.11 2 Corinthians 2. 5-end
Evening Prayer		
Psalm [103;] 105 1 Samuel 1. 1-20 Luke 19. 28-40	Psalm 30; 32 1 Samuel 16. 14-23 Luke 8. 1-3	Psalm 119. 129-152 1 Samuel 2. 12-26 Luke 20. 1-8
... on the eve of Mary Magdalene: *Psalm 139: Isaiah 25. 1-9: 2 Corinthians 1. 3-7*		

Advent 2024 - Kingdom 2025

THIRD SERVICE	SECOND SERVICE	Notes
Psalm 82; 100 Deuteronomy 30. 1-10 1 Peter 3. 8-18	Psalm 81 Genesis 41. 1-16, 25-37 1 Corinthians 4. 8-13 *If the Second Service is a Eucharist, the Gospel is:* John 4. 31-35	1984 BCP page 167. * For the replaced readings, see page 117. † For weekday commemorations see page 139.

Thursday 24 July	* James, Apostle Friday 25 July	† Anne and Joachim Saturday 26 July
	DAILY EUCHARIST	
Collect & PC 91 & 92 Exodus 19. 1-20 Psalm 24. 1-6 Matthew 13. 10-17	Collect & PC 230 & 110 *Either:* Jeremiah 45 Psalm 126 Acts 11.27 – 12.2 Matthew 20. 20-28 *or:* Acts 11.27 – 12.2 Psalm 126 2 Corinthians 4. 7-15 Matthew 20. 20-28	Collect & PC 91 & 92 Exodus 24. 3-8 Psalm 50. 1-15 Matthew 13. 24-30
	Morning Prayer	
Psalm [113;] 115 Ezekiel 3. 12-end 2 Corinthians 3	Psalm 7; 29 2 Kings 1. 9-15 Luke 9. 46-56	Psalm [120;] 121; [122] Ezekiel 9 2 Corinthians 5
	Evening Prayer	
Psalm [114;] 116; [117] 1 Samuel 2. 27-end Luke 20. 9-19	Psalm 94 Jeremiah 26. 1-15 Mark 1. 14-20	Psalm 118 1 Samuel 4. 1b-end Luke 20. 27-40
... on the eve of James: Psalm 144: Deuteronomy 30. 11-20: Mark 5. 21-43		

THE SIXTH SUNDAY *after* TRINITY (Proper 12)

DATE	COLLECT & PC	PRINCIPAL SERVICE	
Sunday 27 July (†)	93 & 94	*Continuous:* Hosea 1. 2-10 Psalm 85 *or* 85. 1-7 Colossians 2. 6-15, [16-19] Luke 11. 1-13	*or Related:* Genesis 18. 20-32 Psalm 138 Colossians 2. 6-15, [16-19] Luke 11. 1-13

† Samson	† William Wilberforce, Josephine Butler and all Social Reformers	† Silas
Monday 28 July	**Tuesday 29 July**	**Wednesday 30 July**
DAILY EUCHARIST		
Collect & PC 93 & 94 Exodus 32. 15-24, 30-34 Psalm 106. 19-23 Matthew 13. 31-35	Collect & PC 93 & 94 Exodus 33. 7-11; 34. 5-10, 27, 28 Psalm 103. 1-13 Matthew 13. 36-43	Collect & PC 93 & 94 Exodus 34. 29-35 Psalm 99 Matthew 13. 44-46
Morning Prayer		
Psalm [123; 124; 125;] 126 Ezekiel 10. 1-19 2 Corinthians 6.1 – 7.1	Psalm 132; [133] Ezekiel 11. 14-end 2 Corinthians 7. 2-end	Psalm 119. 153-end Ezekiel 12. 1-16 2 Corinthians 8. 1-15
Evening Prayer		
Psalm 127; [128; 129] 1 Samuel 5 Luke 20.41 – 21.4	Psalm [134;] 135 1 Samuel 6. 1-16 Luke 21. 5-19	Psalm 136 1 Samuel 7 Luke 21. 20-28

Advent 2024 - Kingdom 2025

THIRD SERVICE	SECOND SERVICE	Notes
Psalm 95 Song of Solomon 2 *or* 1 Maccabees 2. [1-14,] 15-22 1 Peter 4. 7-14	Psalm 88 *or* 88. 1-9 Genesis 42. 1-25 1 Corinthians 10. 1-24 *If the Second Service is a Eucharist, the Gospel is:* **Matthew 13. 24-30, [31-43]**	1984 BCP page 170. † For weekday commemorations see page 139 & 140.

† Joseph of Arimathea

† Ignatius of Loyola

Thursday 31 July	Friday 1 August	Saturday 2 August
DAILY EUCHARIST		
Collect & PC 93 & 94 Exodus 40. 16-21, 34-38 Psalm 84 Matthew 13. 47-53	Collect & PC 93 & 94 Leviticus 23. 1-11, 26-38 Psalm 81. 1-10 Matthew 13. 54-58	Collect & PC 93 & 94 Leviticus 25. 1, 8-17 Psalm 67 Matthew 14. 1-12
Morning Prayer		
Psalm 143; [146] Ezekiel 12. 17-end 2 Corinthians 8.16 – 9.5	Psalm [142;] 144 Ezekiel 13. 1-16 2 Corinthians 9. 6-end	Psalm 147 Ezekiel 14. 1-11 2 Corinthians 10
Evening Prayer		
Psalm 138; [140; 141] 1 Samuel 8 Luke 21. 29-end	Psalm 145 1 Samuel 9. 1-14 Luke 22. 1-13	Psalm 148; [149; 150] 1 Samuel 9.15 – 10.1 Luke 22. 14-23

Year C - Weekdays 1

THE SEVENTH SUNDAY *after* TRINITY (Proper 13)

DATE	COLLECT & PC	PRINCIPAL SERVICE	
Sunday 3 August (†)	95 & 96	*Continuous:* Hosea 11. 1-11 Psalm 107. 1-9, [43] Colossians 3. 1-11 Luke 12. 13-21	*or Related:* Ecclesiastes 1. 2, 12-14; 2. 18-23 Psalm 49. 1-9, [10-12] Colossians 3. 1-11 Luke 12. 13-21

Monday 4 August	† Oswald Tuesday 5 August	* Transfiguration of Our Lord Wednesday 6 August
DAILY EUCHARIST		
Collect & PC 95 & 96 Numbers 11. 4-15 Psalm 81. 10-16 Matthew 14. 22-36	Collect & PC 95 & 96 Numbers 12. 1-17 Psalm 51. 1-11 Matthew 15. 1, 2, 10-14	Collect & PC 239 & 38 Daniel 7. 9, 10, 13, 14 Psalm 97 2 Peter 1. 16-19 Luke 9. 28-36
Morning Prayer		
Psalm 1; [2; 3] Ezekiel 14. 12-end 2 Corinthians 11. 1-15	Psalm 5; [6; 8] Ezekiel 18. 1-20 2 Corinthians 11. 16-end	Psalm 27 Sirach 48. 1-10 or 1 Kings 19. 1-16 1 John 3. 1-3
Evening Prayer		
Psalm 4; [7] 1 Samuel 10. 1-16 Luke 22. 24-30	Psalm 9; [10] 1 Samuel 10. 17-end Luke 22. 31-38	Psalm 72 Exodus 34. 29-35 2 Corinthians 3

... eve of The Transfiguration:
Psalm 99; 110: Exodus 24. 12-18: John 12. 27-36a

Advent 2024 - Kingdom 2025

THIRD SERVICE	SECOND SERVICE	Notes
Psalm 106. 1-10 Song of Solomon 5. 2-16 *or* 1 Maccabees 3. 1-12 2 Peter 1. 1-15	Psalm 107. 1-12, [13-32] Genesis 50. 4-26 1 Corinthians 14. 1-19 *If the Second Service is a Eucharist, the Gospel is:* Mark 6. 45-52	1984 BCP page 172. * For the replaced readings, see page 118. † For weekday commemorations see page 140 & 141.

	† Dominic	† Augustine Baker *or* † Mary Sumner *or* † Edith Stein
Thursday 7 August	**Friday 8 August**	**Saturday 9 August**
\multicolumn{3}{c}{**DAILY EUCHARIST**}		
Collect & PC 95 & 96 Numbers 20. 1-13 Psalm 95. 1-9 Matthew 16. 13-23	Collect & PC 95 & 96 Deuteronomy 4. 32-40 Psalm 77. 11-20 Matthew 16. 24-28	Collect & PC 95 & 96 Deuteronomy 6. 4-13 Psalm 18. 1, 2, 46-50 Matthew 17. 14-20
\multicolumn{3}{c}{**Morning Prayer**}		
Psalm [14;] 15; [16] Ezekiel 20. 1-20 2 Corinthians 13	Psalm [17;] 19 Ezekiel 20. 21-38 James 1. 1-11	Psalm [20; 21;] 23 Ezekiel 24.15–end James 1. 12-end
\multicolumn{3}{c}{**Evening Prayer**}		
Psalm 18 1 Samuel 12 Luke 22. 47-62	Psalm 22 1 Samuel 13. 5-18 Luke 22. 63-end	Psalm 24; [25] 1 Samuel 13.19 – 14.15 Luke 23. 1-12

Year C - Weekdays 1

THE EIGHTH SUNDAY *after* TRINITY (Proper 14)

DATE	COLLECT & PC	PRINCIPAL SERVICE	
Sunday 10 August (†)	97 & 98	*Continuous:* Isaiah 1. 1, 10-20 Psalm 50. 1-8, 22-23 *or* 50. 1-7 Hebrews 11. 1-3, 8-16 Luke 12. 32-40	*or Related:* Genesis 15. 1-6 Psalm 33. 12-21, [22] Hebrews 11. 1-3, 8-16 Luke 12. 32-40

† Clare of Assisi	† Ann Griffiths	† Jeremy Taylor
Monday 11 August	Tuesday 12 August	Wednesday 13 August
DAILY EUCHARIST		
Collect & PC 97 & 98 Deuteronomy 10. 12-22 Psalm 148 Matthew 17. 22-27	Collect & PC 97 & 98 Deuteronomy 31. 1-8 Psalm 111 Matthew 18. 1-5, 10, 12-14	Collect & PC 97 & 98 Deuteronomy 34. 1-12 Psalm 66. 1-9 Matthew 18. 15-20
Morning Prayer		
Psalm [27;] 30 Ezekiel 28. 1-19 James 2. 1-13	Psalm [32;] 36 Ezekiel 33. 1-20 James 2. 14-end	Psalm 34 Ezekiel 33. 21-end James 3
Evening Prayer		
Psalm [26;] 28; [29] 1 Samuel 14. 24-46 Luke 23. 13-25	Psalm 33 1 Samuel 15. 1-23 Luke 23. 26-43	Psalm 119. 33-56 1 Samuel 16 Luke 23. 44-56a

Advent 2024 - Kingdom 2025

THIRD SERVICE	SECOND SERVICE	Notes
Psalm 115 Song of Solomon 8. 5-7 or 1 Maccabees 14. 4-15 2 Peter 3. 8-13	Psalm 108; [116] Isaiah 11.10 – 12.6 2 Corinthians 1. 1-22 *If the Second Service is a Eucharist, the Gospel is:* Mark 7. 24-30	1984 BCP page 174. * For the replaced readings, see page 117. † For weekday commemorations see page (141 &) 142.

† Maximilian Kolbe	* Mary, Mother of Our Lord	
Thursday 14 August	Friday 15 August	Saturday 16 August
DAILY EUCHARIST		
Collect & PC 97 & 98 Joshua 3. 7-17 Psalm 114 Matthew 18.21 – 19.1	Collect & PC 249 & 8 Isaiah 6. 1, 10-11 *or* Revelation 11.19 – 12.6, 10 Psalm 45. 10-17 Galatians 4. 4-7 Luke 1. 46-55	Collect & PC 97 & 98 Joshua 24. 14-29 Psalm 16. 1, 5-11 Matthew 19. 13-15
Morning Prayer		
Psalm 37 Ezekiel 34. 1-16 James 4. 1-12	Psalm 98; 138 Isaiah 7. 10-15 Luke 11. 27, 28	Psalm [41;] 42; [43] Ezekiel 36. 16-36 James 5. 7-end
Evening Prayer		
Psalm [39;] 40 1 Samuel 17. 1-30 Luke 23.56b – 24.12 *... eve of Mary:* Psalm 72: Proverbs 8. 22-31: John 19. 23-27	Psalm 132 Song of Solomon 2. 1-7 Acts 1. 6-14	Psalm [45;] 46 1 Samuel 17.55 – 18.16 Luke 24. 36-end

Year C - Weekdays 1

THE NINTH SUNDAY *after* TRINITY (Proper 15)

DATE	COLLECT & PC	PRINCIPAL SERVICE	
Sunday 17 August	99 & 100	*Continuous:* Isaiah 5. 1-7 Psalm 80. [1, 2,] 8-19 Hebrews 11.29 – 12.2 Luke 12. 49-56	*or Related:* Jeremiah 23. 23-29 Psalm 82 Hebrews 11.29 – 12.2 Luke 12. 49-56

		† Bernard
Monday 18 August	**Tuesday 19 August**	**Wednesday 20 August**
DAILY EUCHARIST		
Collect & PC 99 & 100 Judges 2. 11-19 Psalm 51. 1-9 Matthew 19. 16-22	Collect & PC 99 & 100 Judges 5. 11-24a Psalm 85. 8-13 Matthew 19. 23-30	Collect & PC 99 & 100 Judges 9. 6-15 Psalm 21. 1-7 Matthew 20. 1-16a
Morning Prayer		
Psalm 44 Ezekiel 37. 1-14 Mark 1. 1-13	Psalm 48; [52] Ezekiel 37. 15-end Mark 1. 14-20	Psalm 119. 57-80 Ezekiel 39. 21-end Mark 1. 21-28
Evening Prayer		
Psalm 47; [49] 1 Samuel 19. 1-18 Acts 1. 1-14	Psalm 50 1 Samuel 20. 1-17 Acts 1. 15-end	Psalm 59; [60; 67] 1 Samuel 20. 18-end Acts 2. 1-21

Advent 2024 - Kingdom 2025

THIRD SERVICE	SECOND SERVICE	Notes
Psalm 119. 33-48 Jonah 1 *or* Sirach 3. 1-15 2 Peter 3. 14-18	Psalm 119. 17-24, [25-32] Isaiah 28. 9-22 2 Corinthians 8. 1-9 *If the Second Service is a Eucharist, the Gospel is:* **Matthew 20. 1-16**	1984 BCP page 176. † For weekday commemorations see page 142 & 143.

		† Tydfil
Thursday 21 August	**Friday 22 August**	**Saturday 23 August**
DAILY EUCHARIST		
Collect & PC 99 & 100 Judges 11. 29-40 Psalm 130 Matthew 22. 1-14	Collect & PC 99 & 100 Ruth 1. 1-22 Psalm 146 Matthew 22. 34-40	Collect & PC 99 & 100 Ruth 2. 1-11; 4. 13-17 Psalm 128 Matthew 23. 1-12
Morning Prayer		
Psalm [56;] 57; [63] Ezekiel 43. 1-12 Mark 1. 29-end	Psalm 51; [54] Ezekiel 44. 4-16 Mark 2. 1-12	Psalm 68 Ezekiel 47. 1-12 Mark 2. 13-22
Evening Prayer		
Psalm [61;] 62; [64] 1 Samuel 21.1 – 22.5 Acts 2. 22-36	Psalm 38 1 Samuel 22. 6-end Acts 2. 37-end	Psalm [65;] 66 1 Samuel 23 Acts 3. 1-10

... eve of Bartholomew:
Psalm 97: Isaiah 61. 1-9: 2 Corinthians 6. 1-10

BARTHOLOMEW, APOSTLE

DATE	COLLECT & PC	PRINCIPAL SERVICE	
Sunday 24 August	252 & 110	*Either* Isaiah 43. 8-13 Psalm 145. 1-7 Acts 5. 12-16 Luke 22. 24-30	*or* Acts 5. 12-16 Psalm 145. 1-7 1 Corinthians 4. 9-15 Luke 22. 24-30

		† Monica
Monday 25 August	**Tuesday 26 August**	**Wednesday 27 August**
DAILY EUCHARIST		
Collect & PC 99 & 100 1 Thessalonians 1. 1-10 Psalm 149. 1-5 Matthew 23. 13-22	Collect & PC 99 & 100 1 Thessalonians 2. 1-8 Psalm 139. 1-10 Matthew 23. 23-26	Collect & PC 99 & 100 1 Thessalonians 2. 9-13 Psalm 126 Matthew 23. 27-32
Morning Prayer		
Psalm 71 Proverbs 1. 1-19 Mark 2.23 – 3.6	Psalm 73 Proverbs 1. 20-end Mark 3. 7-19a	Psalm 77 Proverbs 2 Mark 3. 19b-end
Evening Prayer		
Psalm 72; [75] 1 Samuel 24 Acts 3. 11-end	Psalm 74 1 Samuel 26 Acts 4. 1-12	Psalm 119. 81-104 1 Samuel 28. 3-end Acts 4. 13-31

Advent 2024 - Kingdom 2025

THIRD SERVICE	SECOND SERVICE	Notes
Psalm 86 Genesis 28. 10-17 John 1. 43-51	Psalm 91; 116 Sirach 39. 1-10 *or* Deuteronomy 18. 15-19 Matthew 10. 1-22	1984 BCP page 176. † For weekday commemorations see page 143.

† Augustine of Hippo	† The beheading of John the Baptist	
Thursday 28 August	**Friday 29 August**	**Saturday 30 August**
DAILY EUCHARIST		
Collect & PC 99 & 100 1 Thessalonians 3. 6-13 Psalm 90. 13-17 Matthew 24. 42-51	Collect & PC 99 & 100 1 Thessalonians 4. 1-8 Psalm 97 Matthew 25. 1-13	Collect & PC 99 & 100 1 Thessalonians 4. 9-12 Psalm 98 Matthew 25. 14-30
Morning Prayer		
Psalm 78. 1-39 Proverbs 3. 1-26 Mark 4. 1-20	Psalm 55 Proverbs 3.27 – 4.19 Mark 4. 21-34	Psalm 76; [79] Proverbs 6. 1-19 Mark 4. 35-end
Evening Prayer		
Psalm 78. 40-end 1 Samuel 31 Acts 4.32 – 5.11	Psalm 69 2 Samuel 1 Acts 5. 12-26	Psalm [81;] 84 2 Samuel 2. 1-11 Acts 5. 27-end

Year C - Weekdays 1

THE ELEVENTH SUNDAY *after* TRINITY (Proper 17)

DATE	COLLECT & PC	PRINCIPAL SERVICE	
Sunday 31 August (†)	103 & 104	*Continuous:* Jeremiah 2. 4-13 Psalm 81. 1, 10-16 *or* 81. 1-11 Hebrews 13. 1-8, 15-16 Luke 14. 1, 7-14	*or Related:* Sirach 10. 12-18 *or* Proverbs 25. 6-7 Psalm 112 Hebrews 13. 1-8, 15, 16 Luke 14. 1, 7-14

	† Lucian Tapiedi and the Martyrs of Papua New Guinea	† Gregory the Great
Monday 1 September	**Tuesday 2 September**	**Wednesday 3 September**
DAILY EUCHARIST		
Collect & PC 103 & 104 1 Thessalonians 4. 13-18 Psalm 96 Luke 4. 16-30	Collect & PC 103 & 104 1 Thessalonians 5. 1-11 Psalm 27. 1-4, 13, 14 Luke 4. 31-37	Collect & PC 103 & 104 Colossians 1. 1-8 Psalm 34. 9-22 Luke 4. 38-44
Morning Prayer		
Psalm 80; [82] Proverbs 8. 1-21 Mark 5. 1-20	Psalm [87;] 89. 1-18 Proverbs 8. 22-end Mark 5. 21-34	Psalm 119. 105-128 Proverbs 9 Mark 5. 35-end
Evening Prayer		
Psalm [85;] 86 2 Samuel 3. 12-end Acts 6	Psalm 89. 19-end 2 Samuel 5. 1-12 Acts 7. 1-16	Psalm 91; [93] 2 Samuel 6. 1-19 Acts 7. 17-43

Advent 2024 - Kingdom 2025

THIRD SERVICE	SECOND SERVICE	Notes
Psalm 119. 161-176 Jonah 3. 1-9 *or* Sirach 11. [7-17,] 18-28 Revelation 3. 14-22	Psalm 119. 81-88, [89-96] Isaiah 33. 13-22 John 3. 22-36	1984 BCP page 180. † For weekday commemorations see page 144.

Thursday 4 September	Friday 5 September	Saturday 6 September
DAILY EUCHARIST		
Collect & PC 103 & 104 Colossians 1. 9-14 Psalm 98 Luke 5. 1-11	Collect & PC 103 & 104 Colossians 1. 15-20 Psalm 100 Luke 5. 33-39	Collect & PC 103 & 104 Colossians 1. 21-23 Psalm 54 Luke 6. 1-5
Morning Prayer		
Psalm [90;] 92 Proverbs 10. 1-12 Mark 6. 1-13	Psalm 88; [95] Proverbs 11. 1-12 Mark 6. 14-29	Psalm [96;] 97; [100] Proverbs 12. 10-end Mark 6. 30-44
Evening Prayer		
Psalm 94 2 Samuel 7. 1-17 Acts 7. 44-53	Psalm 102 2 Samuel 7. 18-end Acts 7.54 – 8.3	Psalm 104 2 Samuel 9 Acts 8. 4-25

Year C - Weekdays 1

THE TWELFTH SUNDAY *after* TRINITY (Proper 18)

DATE	COLLECT & PC	PRINCIPAL SERVICE	
Sunday 7 September	105 & 106	*Continuous:* Jeremiah 18. 1-11 Psalm 139. 1-6, 13-18 *or* 139. 1-8 Philemon 1-21 Luke 14. 25-33	*or Related:* Deuteronomy 30. 15-20 Psalm 1 Philemon 1-21 Luke 14. 25-33

† The Nativity of the Blessed Virgin Mary		† William Salesbury and William Morgan
Monday 8 September	**Tuesday 9 September**	**Wednesday 10 September**
DAILY EUCHARIST		
Collect & PC 105 & 106	Collect & PC 105 & 106	Collect & PC 105 & 106
Colossians 1.24 – 2.3	Colossians 2. 6-15	Colossians 3. 1-11
Psalm 62. 1-7	Psalm 145. 1-9	Psalm 145. 10-13
Luke 6. 6-11	Luke 6. 12-19	Luke 6. 20-26
Morning Prayer		
Psalm 98; [99; 101]	Psalm 106; [103]	Psalm [110;] 111; [112]
Proverbs 14.31 – 15.17	Proverbs 15. 18-end	Proverbs 18. 10-end
Mark 6. 45-end	Mark 7. 1-13	Mark 7. 14-23
Evening Prayer		
Psalm 105; [103]	Psalm 107	Psalm 119. 129-152
2 Samuel 11	2 Samuel 12. 1-25	2 Samuel 15. 1-12
Acts 8 .26-end	Acts 9. 1-19a	Acts 9. 19b-31

Advent 2024 - Kingdom 2025

THIRD SERVICE	SECOND SERVICE	Notes
Psalm 122; 123 Jonah 3.10 – 4.11 *or* Sirach 27.30 – 28.9 Revelation 8. 1-5	Psalm [120;] 121 Isaiah 43.14 – 44.5 John 5. 30-47	1984 BCP page 183. † For weekday commemorations see page 144.

† Deiniol		† Cyprian
Thursday 11 September	**Friday 12 September**	**Saturday 13 September**
DAILY EUCHARIST		
Collect & PC 105 & 106 Colossians 3. 12-17 Psalm 150 Luke 6. 27-38	Collect & PC 105 & 106 1 Timothy 1. 1, 2, 12-14 Psalm 16 Luke 6. 39-42	Collect & PC 105 & 106 1 Timothy 1. 15-17 Psalm 113 Luke 6. 43-49
Morning Prayer		
Psalm [113;] 115 Proverbs 20. 1-22 Mark 7. 24-30	Psalm 139 Proverbs 22. 1-16 Mark 7. 31-end	Psalm [120;] 121; [122] Proverbs 24. 23-end Mark 8. 1-10
Evening Prayer		
Psalm [114]; 116; [117] 2 Samuel 15. 13-end Acts 9. 32-end	Psalm 130; [131; 137] 2 Samuel 16. 1-14 Acts 10. 1-16	Psalm 118 2 Samuel 17. 1-23 Acts 10. 17-33
	... eve of Holy Cross: *Psalm 66: Isaiah 52.13 – 53.12: Ephesians 2. 11-22*	

Year C - Weekdays 1

HOLY CROSS

DATE	COLLECT & PC	PRINCIPAL SERVICE
Sunday 14 September	265 & 54	Numbers 21. 4-9 Psalm 22. 23-28 Philippians 2. 6-11 John 3. 13-17
Education Sunday		

† Ninian

Monday 15 September	Tuesday 16 September	Wednesday 17 September
DAILY EUCHARIST		
Collect & PC 107 & 108 1 Timothy 2. 1-8 Psalm 28 Luke 7. 1-10	Collect & PC 107 & 108 1 Timothy 3. 1-13 Psalm 101 Luke 7. 11-17	Collect & PC 107 & 108 1 Timothy 3. 14-16 Psalm 111. 1-6 Luke 7. 31-35
Morning Prayer		
Psalm [123; 124; 125;] 126 Proverbs 25. 1-14 Mark 8. 11-21	Psalm 132; [133] Proverbs 25. 15-end Mark 8. 22-26	Psalm 119. 153-end Proverbs 26. 12-end Mark 8.27 – 9.1
Evening Prayer		
Psalm 127; [128; 129] 2 Samuel 18. 1-18 Acts 10. 34-end	Psalm [134,] 135 2 Samuel 18.19 – 19.8a Acts 11. 1-18	Psalm 136 2 Samuel 19. 8b-23 Acts 11. 19-end

Advent 2024 - Kingdom 2025

THIRD SERVICE	SECOND SERVICE	Notes
Psalm 2; 8 Genesis 3. 1-15 John 12. 27-36a	Psalm 110; 150 Isaiah 63. 1-16 1 Corinthians 1. 18-25	1984 BCP page 185. † For weekday commemorations see page 145.

		† Saints, Martyrs & Missionaries of Australasia and the Pacific
Thursday 18 September	Friday 19 September	Saturday 20 September
DAILY EUCHARIST		
Collect & PC 107 & 108 1 Timothy 4. 12-16 Psalm 111. 7-10 Luke 7. 36-50	Collect & PC 107 & 108 1 Timothy 6. 1-12 Psalm 49. 1-9 Luke 8. 1-3	Collect & PC 107 & 108 1 Timothy 6. 13-16 Psalm 100 Luke 8. 4-15
Morning Prayer		
Psalm 143; [146] Proverbs 27. 1-22 Mark 9. 2-13	Psalm [142;] 144 Proverbs 30. 1-9, 24-31 Mark 9. 14-29	Psalm 147 Proverbs 31. 10-end Mark 9. 30-37
Evening Prayer		
Psalm 138; [140; 141] 2 Samuel 19. 24-end Acts 12. 1-17	Psalm 145 2 Samuel 23. 1-7 Acts 12. 18-end	Psalm 148; [149; 150] 2 Samuel 24 Acts 13. 1-12

... eve of Matthew:
Psalm 34: Isaiah 33. 13-17: Matthew 6. 19-34

Year C - Weekdays 1

MATTHEW, APOSTLE AND EVANGELIST

DATE	COLLECT & PC	PRINCIPAL SERVICE
Sunday 21 September	268 & 127	Proverbs 3. 13-18 Psalm 119. 65-72 2 Corinthians 4. 1-6 Matthew 9. 9-13

		Ember Day † Sergei of Radonezh
Monday 22 September	**Tuesday 23 September**	**Wednesday 24 September**
DAILY EUCHARIST		
Collect & PC 109 & 110 Ezra 1. 1-6 Psalm 126 Luke 8. 16-18	Collect & PC 109 & 110 Ezra 6. 1-8, 12-19 Psalm 124 Luke 8. 19-21	Collect & PC 351 & 352 Ember set 1, 2 *or* 3. See page 150.
Morning Prayer		
Psalm 1; [2; 3] Wisdom 1 *or* 1 Chronicles 10.1 – 11.9 Mark 9. 38-end	Psalm 5; [6; 8] Wisdom 2 *or* 1 Chronicles 13 Mark 10. 1-16	Psalm 119. 1-32 Wisdom 3. 1-9 *or* 1 Chronicles 15.1 – 16.3 Mark 10. 17-31
Evening Prayer		
Psalm 4; [7] 1 Kings 1. 5-31 Acts 13. 13-43	Psalm 9; [10] 1 Kings 1.32 – 2.4, 10-12 Acts 13.44 – 14.7	Psalm 11; [12; 13] 1 Kings 3 Acts 14 .8-end

Advent 2024 - Kingdom 2025

THIRD SERVICE	SECOND SERVICE	Notes
Psalm 49 1 Kings 19. 15-21 2 Timothy 3. 14-17	Psalm 119. 33-40, 89-96 Ecclesiastes 5. 4-12 Matthew 19. 16-30	1984 BCP page 187. † For weekday commemorations see page 145 & 146.

	Ember Day	Ember Day
† Cadoc	† Lancelot Andrewes	† Vincent de Paul
Thursday 25 September	**Friday 26 September**	**Saturday 27 September**
DAILY EUCHARIST		
Collect & PC 109 & 110 Haggai 1. 1-8 Psalm 149. 1-5 Luke 9. 7-9	Collect & PC 351 & 352 Ember set 1, 2 *or* 3. See page 150.	Collect & PC 351 & 352 Ember set 1, 2 *or* 3. See page 150.
Morning Prayer		
Psalm [14;] 15; [16] Wisdom 4. 7-end *or* 1 Chronicles 17 Mark 10. 32-34	Psalm [17;] 19 Wisdom 5. 1-16 *or* 1 Chronicles 21.1 – 22.1 Mark 10. 35-45	Psalm [20; 21;] 23 Wisdom 5.17 – 6.11 *or* 1 Chronicles 22. 2-end Mark 10. 46-end
Evening Prayer		
Psalm 18 1 Kings 4.29 – 5.12 Acts 15. 1-21	Psalm 22 1 Kings 6. 1, 11-28 Acts 15. 22-35	Psalm 24; [25] 1 Kings 8. 1-30 Acts 15.36 – 16.5

Year C - Weekdays 1

THE FIFTEENTH SUNDAY *after* TRINITY (Proper 21)

DATE	COLLECT & PC	PRINCIPAL SERVICE	
Sunday 28 September	111 & 112	*Continuous:* Jeremiah 32. 1-3a, 6-15 Psalm 91. 1-6, 14-16 *or* 91. 11-16 1 Timothy 6. 6-19 Luke 16. 19-31	*or Related:* Amos 6. 1a, 4-7 Psalm 146 1 Timothy 6. 6-19 Luke 16. 19-31

* Michael and All Angels Monday 29 September	† Jerome Tuesday 30 September	Wednesday 1 October
DAILY EUCHARIST		
Collect & PC 272 & 273 *Either:* Genesis 28. 10-17 Psalm 103. 19-22 Revelation 12. 7-12 John 1. 47-51 *or:* Revelation 12. 7-12 Psalm 103. 19-22 Hebrews 1. 5-14 John 1. 47-51	Collect & PC 111 & 112 Zechariah 8. 20-23 Psalm 87 Luke 9. 51-56	Collect & PC 111 & 112 Nehemiah 2. 1-8 Psalm 137. 1-6 Luke 9. 57-62
Morning Prayer		
Psalm 34 Tobit 12. 6-22 *or* Daniel 12. 1-4 Acts 12. 1-11	Psalm [32;] 36 Wisdom 7. 1-14 *or* 1 Chronicles 28. 11-end Mark 11. 12-26	Psalm 34 Wisdom 7.15 – 8.4 *or* 1 Chronicles 29. 1-9 Mark 11. 27-end
Evening Prayer		
Psalm 138; 148 Daniel 10. 4-21 Revelation 5	Psalm 33 1 Kings 8.63 – 9.9 Acts 16. 25-end	Psalm 119. 33-56 1 Kings 10. 1-25 Acts 17. 1-15

Advent 2024 - Kingdom 2025

THIRD SERVICE	SECOND SERVICE	Notes
Psalm 132 Isaiah 48. 12-22 Luke 11. 37-54	Psalm 134; 135 *or* 135. 1-14 Nehemiah 2 John 8. 31-38, 48-59	1984 BCP page 190. * For the replaced readings, see page 118. † For weekday commemorations see page 146.

Evening Prayer on the eve of Michael:
Psalm 91: 2 Kings 6. 8-17: Matthew 18. 1-6, 10

† Francis of Assisi

Thursday 2 October	Friday 3 October	Saturday 4 October
\multicolumn{3}{c}{DAILY EUCHARIST}		
Collect & PC 111 & 112 Nehemiah 8. 1-12 Psalm 19. 7-10 Luke 10. 1-12	Collect & PC 111 & 112 Baruch 1. 15-21 Psalm 79. 1-9 Luke 10. 13-16	Collect & PC 111 & 112 Baruch 4. 5-12, 27-29 Psalm 69. 32-36 Luke 10. 17-24
Morning Prayer		
Psalm 37 Wisdom 8. 5-18 *or* 1 Chronicles 29. 10-20 Mark 12. 1-12	Psalm 31 Wisdom 8.21 – *end of* 9 *or* 1 Chronicles 29. 21-end Mark 12. 13-17	Psalm [41;] 42; [43] Wisdom 10.15 – 11.10 *or* 2 Chronicles 1. 1-13 Mark 12. 18-27
Evening Prayer		
Psalm [39;] 40 1 Kings 11. 1-13 Acts 17. 16-end	Psalm 35 1 Kings 11. 26-end Acts 18. 1-21	Psalm [45;] 46 1 Kings 12. 1-24 Acts 18.22 – 19.7

Year C - Weekdays 1

THE SIXTEENTH SUNDAY *after* TRINITY (Proper 22)

DATE	COLLECT & PC	PRINCIPAL SERVICE	
Sunday 5 October	113 & 114	*Continuous:* Lamentations 1. 1-6 *Canticle:* Lamentations 3. 19-26 *or* Psalm 137 *or* 137. 1-6 2 Timothy 1. 1-14 Luke 17. 5-10	*or Related:* Habakkuk 1. 1-4; 2. 1-4 Psalm 37. 1-9 2 Timothy 1. 1-14 Luke 17. 5-10

† William Tyndale

Monday 6 October	Tuesday 7 October	Wednesday 8 October
DAILY EUCHARIST		
Collect & PC 113 & 114 Jonah 1. 1-17; 2. 10 Psalm 130 Luke 10. 25-37	Collect & PC 113 & 114 Jonah 3. 1-10 Psalm 6 Luke 10. 38-42	Collect & PC 113 & 114 Jonah 4. 1-11 Psalm 86. 1-10 Luke 11. 1-4
Morning Prayer		
Psalm 44 Wisdom 11.21 – 12.2 *or* 2 Chronicles 2. 1-16 Mark 12. 28-34	Psalm 48; [52] Wisdom 12. 12-21 *or* 2 Chronicles 3 Mark 12. 35-end	Psalm 119. 57-80 Wisdom 13. 1-9 *or* 2 Chronicles 5 Mark 13. 1-13
Evening Prayer		
Psalm 47; [49] 1 Kings 12.25 – 13.10 Acts 19. 8-20	Psalm 50 1 Kings 13. 11-end Acts 19. 21-end	Psalm 59; [60; 67] 1 Kings 17 Acts 20. 1-16

Advent 2024 - Kingdom 2025

THIRD SERVICE	SECOND SERVICE	Notes
Psalm 141 Isaiah 49. 13-23 Luke 12. 1-12	Psalm 142 Nehemiah 5. 1-13 John 9	1984 BCP page 192. † For weekday commemorations see page 146.
Thanksgiving for the Harvest (traditionally around the first Sunday of October). The readings may be used at the Eucharist or a Non-Eucharistic service. See page 155.		

† Cynog

Thursday 9 October	Friday 10 October	Saturday 11 October
DAILY EUCHARIST		
Collect & PC 113 & 114 Malachi 3.13 – 4.2a Psalm 1 Luke 11. 5-13	Collect & PC 113 & 114 Joel 1. 13-15; 2. 1, 2 Psalm 9. 1-8 Luke 11. 14-26	Collect & PC 113 & 114 Joel 3. 12-21 Psalm 97 Luke 11. 27, 28
Morning Prayer		
Psalm [56;] 57; [63] Wisdom 16.15 – 17.1 or 2 Chronicles 6. 1-21 Mark 13. 14-23	Psalm 51; [54] Wisdom 18. 6-19 or 2 Chronicles 6. 22-end Mark 13. 24-31	Psalm 68 Wisdom 19 or 2 Chronicles 7 Mark 13. 32-end
Evening Prayer		
Psalm [61;] 62; [64] 1 Kings 18. 1-20 Acts 20. 17-end	Psalm 38 1 Kings 18. 21-end Acts 21. 1-16	Psalm [65;] 66 1 Kings 19 Acts 21. 17-36

Year C - Weekdays 1

THE SEVENTEENTH SUNDAY *after* TRINITY (Proper 23)

DATE	COLLECT & PC	PRINCIPAL SERVICE	
Sunday 12 October Homelessness Sunday and Prisoners' Sunday and week	115 & 116	*Continuous:* Jeremiah 29. 1, 4-7 Psalm 66. 1-12 2 Timothy 2. 8-15 Luke 17. 11-19	*or Related:* 2 Kings 5. 1-3, 7-15c Psalm 111 2 Timothy 2. 8-15 Luke 17. 11-19

† Edward the Confessor	† Esther John	† Teresa of Avila
Monday 13 October	**Tuesday 14 October**	**Wednesday 15 October**
DAILY EUCHARIST		
Collect & PC 115 & 116 Romans 1. 1-7 Psalm 98 Luke 11. 29-32	Collect & PC 115 & 116 Romans 1. 16-25 Psalm 19. 1-4 Luke 11. 37-41	Collect & PC 115 & 116 Romans 2. 1-11 Psalm 62. 1-8 Luke 11. 42-46
Morning Prayer		
Psalm 71 1 Maccabees 1. 1-19 *or* 2 Chronicles 9. 1-12 Mark 14. 1-11	Psalm 73 1 Maccabees 1. 20-40 *or* 2 Chronicles 10.1 – 11.4 Mark 14. 12-25	Psalm 77 1 Maccabees 1. 41-end *or* 2 Chronicles 12 Mark 14. 26-42
Evening Prayer		
Psalm 72; [75] 1 Kings 21 Acts 21.37 – 22.21	Psalm 74 1 Kings 22. 1-28 Acts 22.22 – 23.11	Psalm 119. 81-104 1 Kings 22. 29-45 Acts 23. 12-end

Advent 2024 - Kingdom 2025

THIRD SERVICE	SECOND SERVICE	Notes
Psalm 143 Isaiah 50. 4-10 Luke 13. 22-30	Psalm 144 Nehemiah 6. 1-16 John 15. 12-27	1984 BCP page 194. * For the replaced readings, see page 118. † For weekday commemorations see page 147.

† Daniel Rowland	† Ignatius	* Luke, Evangelist
Thursday 16 October	Friday 17 October	Saturday 18 October
DAILY EUCHARIST		
Collect & PC 115 & 116 Romans 3. 21-31 Psalm 130 Luke 11. 47-54	Collect & PC 115 & 116 Romans 4. 1-8 Psalm 32 Luke 12. 1-7	Collect & PC 283 & 284 Isaiah 35. 3-6 *or* Acts 16. 6-12a Psalm 147. 1-7 2 Timothy 4. 5-17 Luke 10. 1-9
Morning Prayer		
Psalm 78. 1-39 1 Maccabees 2. 1-28 *or* 2 Chronicles 13.1 – 14.1 Mark 14. 43-52	Psalm 55 1 Maccabees 2. 29-48 *or* 2 Chronicles 14. 2-end Mark 14. 53-65	Psalm 145 Isaiah 55 Luke 1. 1-4
Evening Prayer		
Psalm 78. 40-end 2 Kings 1. 2-17 Acts 24. 1-23	Psalm 69 2 Kings 2. 1-18 Acts 24.24 – 25.12	Psalm 103 Sirach 38. 1-14 *or* Isaiah 61. 1-6 Colossians 4. 7-18

... eve of Luke:
Psalm 33: Hosea 6. 1-3: 2 Timothy 3. 10-17

THE EIGHTEENTH SUNDAY *after* TRINITY (Proper 24)

DATE	COLLECT & PC	PRINCIPAL SERVICE	
Sunday 19 October (†)	117 & 118	*Continuous:* Jeremiah 31. 27-34 Psalm 119. 97-104 2 Timothy 3.14 – 4.5 Luke 18. 1-8	*or Related:* Genesis 32. 22-31 Psalm 121 2 Timothy 3.14 – 4.5 Luke 18. 1-8

Monday 20 October	Tuesday 21 October	Wednesday 22 October
DAILY EUCHARIST		
Collect & PC 117 & 118 Romans 4. 13, 19-25 Psalm 89. 19-29 Luke 12. 13-21	Collect & PC 117 & 118 Romans 5. 6-21 Psalm 40. 6-11 Luke 12. 35-38	Collect & PC 117 & 118 Romans 6. 12-18 Psalm 124 Luke 12. 39-48
Morning Prayer		
Psalm 80; [82] 1 Maccabees 3. 1-26 *or* 2 Chronicles 17. 1-12 Mark 15. 1-15	Psalm [87;] 89. 1-18 1 Maccabees 3. 27-41 *or* 2 Chronicles 18. 1-27 Mark 15. 16-32	Psalm 119. 105-128 1 Maccabees 3. 42-end *or* 2 Chron. 18.28 – *end of* 19 Mark 15. 33-41
Evening Prayer		
Psalm [85;] 86 2 Kings 5 Acts 26. 1-23	Psalm 89. 19-end 2 Kings 6. 1-23 Acts 26. 24-end	Psalm 91; [93] 2 Kings 9. 1-16 Acts 27. 1-26

THIRD SERVICE	SECOND SERVICE	Notes
Psalm 147 Isaiah 54. 1-14 Luke 13. 31-35	Psalm [146;] 149 Nehemiah 8. 9-18 John 16. 1-11	1984 BCP page 196. † For weekday commemorations see page 148.

† James of Jerusalem		† Lewis Bayly
Thursday 23 October	Friday 24 October	Saturday 25 October
DAILY EUCHARIST		
Collect & PC 117 & 118 Romans 6. 19-23 Psalm 1 Luke 12. 49-53	Collect & PC 117 & 118 Romans 7. 18-25a Psalm 119. 33-40 Luke 12. 54-59	Collect & PC 117 & 118 Romans 8. 1-11 Psalm 24. 1-6 Luke 13. 1-9
Morning Prayer		
Psalm [90;] 92 1 Maccabees 4. 1-25 *or* 2 Chronicles 20. 1-23 Mark 15. 42-end	Psalm 88; [95] 1 Maccabees 4. 26-35 *or* 2 Chron. 22.10 – *end of* 23 Mark 16. 1-8	Psalm [96;] 97; [100] 1 Maccabees 4. 36-end *or* 2 Chronicles 24. 1-22 Mark 16. 9-end
Evening Prayer		
Psalm 94 2 Kings 9. 17-end Acts 27. 27-end	Psalm 102 2 Kings 12. 1-19 Acts 28. 1-16	Psalm 104 2 Kings 17. 1-23 Acts 28. 17-end

Year C - Weekdays 1

THE LAST SUNDAY *after* TRINITY *or* BIBLE SUNDAY (Proper 25)

DATE	COLLECT & PC	PRINCIPAL SERVICE	
Sunday 26 October (†)	126 & 127	*Continuous:* Joel 2. 23-32 Psalm 65 *or* 65. 1-8 2 Timothy 4. 6-8, 16-18 Luke 18. 9-14	*or Related:* Sirach 35. 12-17 *or* Jeremiah 14. 7-10, 19-22 Psalm 84. 1-7 2 Timothy 4. 6-8. 16-18 Luke 18. 9-14
BIBLE SUNDAY	126 & 127	Isaiah 45. 22-25 Psalm 119. 129-136	Romans 15. 1-6 Luke 4. 16-24

Monday 27 October	* Simon and Jude, Apostles Tuesday 28 October	Wednesday 29 October
DAILY EUCHARIST		
Collect & PC 126 & 127 Romans 8. 12-17 Psalm 68. 1-6, 19, 20 Luke 13. 10-17	Collect & PC 289 & 110 Isaiah 28. 14-16 Psalm 119. 89-96 Ephesians 2. 19-22 John 15. 17-27	Collect & PC 126 & 127 Romans 8. 26-30 Psalm 13 Luke 13. 22-30
Morning Prayer		
Psalm 98; [99; 101] 1 Maccabees 6. 1-17 *or* 2 Chronicles 26. 1-21 John 13. 1-11	Psalm 116 Wisdom 5. 1-16 *or* Isaiah 45. 18-26 Luke 6. 12-16	Psalm [110;] 111; [112] 1 Maccabees 7. 1-20 *or* 2 Chronicles 29. 1-19 John 13. 21-30
Evening Prayer		
Psalm 105 *or* 103 2 Kings 17. 24-end Philippians 1. 1-11	Psalm 119. 1-16 1 Maccabees 2. 42-66 *or* Jeremiah 3. 11-18 Jude 1-4, 17-25	Psalm 119. 129-152 2 Kings 18. 13-end Philippians 2. 1-13

... on eve of Simon and Jude: Psalm 124; 125; 126: Deuteronomy 32. 1-4: John 14. 15-26

Advent 2024 - Kingdom 2025

THIRD SERVICE	SECOND SERVICE	Notes
Psalm 119. 105-128 Isaiah 59. 9-20 Luke 14. 1-14	Psalm 119. 1-16 Ecclesiastes 11, 12 2 Timothy 2. 1-7 *If the Second Service is a Eucharist, the Gospel is:* **Matthew 22. 34-46**	1984 BCP page 199 Trinty 19. * For the replaced readings, see page 119. † For weekday commemorations see page (148 &) 149.
Psalm 119. 105-128 1 Kings 22. 1-17 Romans 15. 4-13 *or* Luke 14. 1-14	Psalm 119. 1-16 Jeremiah 36. 9-32 Romans 10. 5-17	*If the Second Service is a Eucharist, the Gospel is:* **Matthew 22. 34-40**

† Richard Hooker	† Catholic and Protestant Saints and Martyrs of the Reformation Era *or* Vigil of All Saints	* ALL SAINTS (C) All Saints' Day may be celebrated on the First Sunday of the Kingdom. See page 113.
Thursday 30 October	Friday 31 October	Saturday 1 November

DAILY EUCHARIST

Collect & PC 126 & 127 Romans 8. 31-39 Psalm 30 Luke 13. 31-35	Collect & PC 126 & 127 Romans 9. 1-5 Psalm 147. 12-20 Luke 14. 1-6	Collect & PC 128 & 129 Daniel 7. 1-3, 15-18 Psalm 149 Ephesians 1. 11-23 Luke 6. 20-31

Morning Prayer

Psalm [113;] 115 1 Maccabees 7. 21-end *or* 2 Chronicles 29. 20-end John 13. 31-end	Psalm 139 1 Maccabees 9. 1-22 *or* 2 Chronicles 30 John 14. 1-14	Psalm 15; 84 Isaiah 35. 1-9 Luke 9. 18-27

Evening Prayer

Psalm [114;] 116; [117] 2 Kings 19. 1-19 Philippians 2. 14-end	Psalm 130; [131; 137] 2 Kings 19. 20-36 Philippians 3.1 – 4.1	Psalm 148; 150 Isaiah 65. 17-25 Hebrews 11.32 – 12.2

... eve of All Saints: Psalm 1; 5; Sirach 44. 1-15 or Isaiah 40. 27-31: Revelation 19. 6-10

Year C - Weekdays 1

THE FIRST SUNDAY of THE KINGDOM

DATE	COLLECT & PC	PRINCIPAL SERVICE
Sunday 2 November (†)	131 & 132	Isaiah 1. 10-18 Psalm 32. 1-7 2 Thessalonians 1. 1-12 Luke 19. 1-10

All Saints' Day may be celebrated today, see page 113.

(†) All Souls Monday 3 November (from 2 November)	† Saints and Martyrs of the Anglican Communion Tuesday 4 November	† Cybi Wednesday 5 November
DAILY EUCHARIST		
Collect & PC 293 & 389 Lamentations 3. 17-26 or Wisdom 3. 1-9 Psalm 23 or 27. 1-5, 13, 14 Romans 5. 5-11 or 1 Peter 1. 3-9 John 5. 19-25 or John 6. 37-40	Collect & PC 131 & 132 Romans 12. 1-16 Psalm 131 Luke 14. 15-24	Collect & PC 131 & 132 Romans 13. 8-10 Psalm 112 Luke 14. 25-33
Morning Prayer		
Psalm 31 Judith 15. 1-13 or Leviticus 25. 1-24 Titus 3	Psalm 5; [147. 1-12] Isaiah 1. 21-end Matthew 2. 1-15	Psalm 9; [147. 13-end] Isaiah 2. 1-11 Matthew 2. 16-end
Evening Prayer		
Psalm 35 Sirach 51. 1-12 or Ecclesiastes 11. 1-8 John 20.11–18	Psalm [98; 99;] 100 Daniel 2. 1-24 Revelation 2. 1-11	Psalm [111;] 112; [116] Daniel 2. 25-end Revelation 2. 12-end

Advent 2024 - Kingdom 2025

THIRD SERVICE	SECOND SERVICE	Notes
Colour Variation: Red can be used for The Kingdom Season		
Psalm 87 Job 19. 21-27a Colossians 1. 9-14	Psalm 145 *or* 145. 1-9 Lamentations 3. 22-33 John 11. [1-31,] 32-44	1984 BCP page 201 Trinity 20. † For weekday commemorations see page 149 & 150.

† Illtud	† Richard Davies	† The Saints of Wales
Thursday 6 November	**Friday 7 November**	**Saturday 8 November**
DAILY EUCHARIST		
Collect & PC 131 & 132 Romans 14. 7-12 Psalm 27. 1-4, 13, 14 Luke 15. 1-10	Collect & PC 131 & 132 Romans 15. 14-21 Psalm 98 Luke 16. 1-8	Collect & PC 131 & 132 Romans 16. 3-9, 16, 22-27 Psalm 145. 1-7 Luke 16. 9-15
Morning Prayer		
Psalm [11;] 15; [148] Isaiah 2. 12-end Matthew 3	Psalm 16; [149] Isaiah 3. 1-15 Matthew 4. 1-11	Psalm 18. 31-end; [150] Isaiah 4.2 – 5.7 Matthew 4. 12-22
Evening Prayer		
Psalm 118 Daniel 3. 1-18 Revelation 3. 1-13	Psalm [137; 138;] 143 Daniel 3. 19-end Revelation 3. 14-end	Psalm 145 Daniel 4. 1-18 Revelation 4

Year C - Weekdays 1

THE SECOND SUNDAY *of* THE KINGDOM

DATE	COLLECT & PC	PRINCIPAL SERVICE
Sunday 9 November	134 & 135	Job 19. 23-27a Psalm 17. 1-8, [9] 2 Thessalonians 2. 1-5, 13-17 Luke 20. 27-38
Remembrance Sunday		

† Leo	† Martin	† Tysilio
Monday 10 November	Tuesday 11 November	Wednesday 12 November
DAILY EUCHARIST		
Collect & PC 134 & 135 Wisdom 1. 1-7 Psalm 139. 1-10 Luke 17. 1-6	Collect & PC 134 & 135 Wisdom 2.23 – 3.9 Psalm 34. 15-22 Luke 17. 7-10	Collect & PC 134 & 135 Wisdom 6. 1-11 Psalm 82 Luke 17. 11-19
Morning Prayer		
Psalm [19]; 20 Isaiah 5. 8-24 Matthew 4.23 – 5.12	Psalm 21; [24] Isaiah 5. 25-end Matthew 5. 13-20	Psalm 23; [25] Isaiah 6 Matthew 5. 21-37
Evening Prayer		
Psalm 34 Daniel 4. 19-end Revelation 5	Psalm [36;] 40 Daniel 5. 1-12 Revelation 6	Psalm 37 Daniel 5. 13-end Revelation 7. 1-4, 9-end

Advent 2024 - Kingdom 2025

	Colour Variation: Red can be used for The Kingdom Season	
THIRD SERVICE	SECOND SERVICE	Notes
Psalm 20; 90 Isaiah 2. 1-5 James 3. 13-18	Psalm 40 1 Kings 3. 1-15 Romans 8. 31-39 *If the Second Service is a Eucharist, the Gospel is:* **Matthew 22. 15-22**	1984 BCP page 204 Trinity 21. † For weekday commemorations see page 150 & 151.

† Charles Simeon	† Dyfrig	† The Saints, Martyrs and Missionaries of North America
Thursday 13 November	Friday 14 November	Saturday 15 November
DAILY EUCHARIST		
Collect & PC 134 & 135 Wisdom 7.21 – 8.1 Psalm 119. 89-96 Luke 17. 20-25	Collect & PC 134 & 135 Wisdom 13. 1-9 Psalm 19. 1-4 Luke 17. 26-37	Collect & PC 134 & 135 Wisdom 18. 14-16; 19. 6-9 Psalm 105. 1-6, 37-45 Luke 18. 1-8
Morning Prayer		
Psalm 26; [27] Isaiah 7. 1-17 Matthew 5. 38-end	Psalm [28;] 32 Isaiah 8. 1-15 Matthew 6. 1-18	Psalm 33 Isaiah 8.16 – 9.7 Matthew 6. 19-end
Evening Prayer		
Psalm [42;] 43 Daniel 6 Revelation 8	Psalm 31 Daniel 7. 1-14 Revelation 9. 1-12	Psalm [84;] 86 Daniel 7. 15-end Revelation 9. 13-end

THE THIRD SUNDAY *of* THE KINGDOM

DATE	COLLECT & PC	PRINCIPAL SERVICE
Sunday 16 November (†)	137 & 138	Malachi 4. 1-2a Psalm 98 2 Thessalonians 3. 6-13 Luke 21. 5-19
Safeguarding Sunday		

† Hugh	† Hilda	† Elizabeth of Hungary
Monday 17 November	Tuesday 18 November	Wednesday 19 November
DAILY EUCHARIST		
Collect & PC 137 & 138 1 Maccabees 1. 1-15, 54-57, 62-64 Psalm 79 Luke 18. 35-43	Collect & PC 137 & 138 2 Maccabees 6. 18-31 Psalm 3 Luke 19. 1-10	Collect & PC 137 & 138 2 Maccabees 7. 1, 20-31, 39-42 Psalm 17. 1-8 Luke 19. 11-28
Morning Prayer		
Psalm [46;] 47 Isaiah 9.8 – 10.4 Matthew 7. 1-12	Psalm [48;] 52 Isaiah 10. 5-19 Matthew 7. 13-end	Psalm 56; [57] Isaiah 10. 20-32 Matthew 8. 1-13
Evening Prayer		
Psalm [70;] 71 Daniel 8. 1-14 Revelation 10	Psalm 67; [72] Daniel 8. 15-end Revelation 11. 1-14	Psalm 73 Daniel 9. 1-19 Revelation 11. 15-end

Advent 2024 - Kingdom 2025

Colour Variation: Red can be used for The Kingdom Season		
THIRD SERVICE	SECOND SERVICE	Notes
Psalm 132 1 Samuel 16. 1-13 Matthew 13. 44-52	Psalm [93;] 97 Daniel 6 Matthew 13. 1-9, 18-23	1984 BCP page 207 Trinity 22. † For weekday commemorations see page (151 &) 152.

	† Paulinus of Wales	† Cecilia
Thursday 20 November	**Friday 21 November**	**Saturday 22 November**
DAILY EUCHARIST		
Collect & PC 137 & 138 1 Maccabees 2. 15-29 Psalm 129 Luke 19. 41-44	Collect & PC 137 & 138 1 Maccabees 4. 36, 37, 52-59 Psalm 113 or 122 Luke 19. 45-48	Collect & PC 137 & 138 1 Maccabees 6. 1-13 Psalm 124 Luke 20. 27-40
Morning Prayer		
Psalm [61;] 62 Isaiah 10.33 – 11.9 Matthew 8. 14-22	Psalm 63; [65] Isaiah 11.10 – *end of* 12 Matthew 8. 23-end	Psalm 78. 1-39 Isaiah 13. 1-13 Matthew 9. 1-17
Evening Prayer		
Psalm [74;] 76 Daniel 9. 20-end Revelation 12	Psalm 77 Daniel 10.1 – 11.1 Revelation 13. 1-10	Psalm 78. 40-end Daniel 12 Revelation 13. 11-end
	Alternative for the eve of Christ the King: *Psalm 99; 100: Isaiah 10.33 – 11.9: 1 Timothy 6. 11-16*	

Year C - Weekdays 1

CHRIST THE KING - THE FOURTH SUNDAY *of* THE KINGDOM

DATE	COLLECT & PC	PRINCIPAL SERVICE
Sunday 23 November (†)	140 & 141	Jeremiah 23. 1-6 Psalm 46 Colossians 1. 11-20 Luke 23. 33-43

† John Donne

Monday 24 November	Tuesday 25 November	Wednesday 26 November
DAILY EUCHARIST		
Collect & PC 140 & 141 Daniel 1. 1-20 Psalm 24. 1-6 Luke 21. 1-4	Collect & PC 140 & 141 Daniel 2. 31-45 Psalm 96 Luke 21. 5-9	Collect & PC 140 & 141 Daniel 5. 1-6, 13-28 Psalm 98 Luke 21. 10-19
Morning Prayer		
Psalm [92;] 96 Isaiah 14. 3-20 Matthew 9. 18-34	Psalm 97; [98; 100] Isaiah 17 Matthew 9.35 – 10.15	Psalm [110; 111;] 112 Isaiah 19 Matthew 10. 16-33
Evening Prayer		
Psalm 80; [81] Isaiah 40. 1-11 Revelation 14. 1-13	Psalm [99;] 101 Isaiah 40. 12-26 Rev. 14.14 – *end of* 15	Psalm [121;] 122; [123; 124] Isaiah 40.27 – 41.7 Revelation 16. 1-11

Advent 2024 - Kingdom 2025

THIRD SERVICE	SECOND SERVICE	Notes
Psalm 29; 110 Zechariah 6. 9-15 Revelation 11. 15-18	Psalm 72 *or* 72. 1-7 1 Samuel 8. 4-20 John 18. 33-37	1984 BCP page 216 Sunday before Advent. † For weekday commemorations see page 153 & 122.

† Vigil and Day of Intercession for the Mission of the Church

Thursday 27 November	Friday 28 November	Saturday 29 November
DAILY EUCHARIST		
Collect & PC 140 & 141 Daniel 6. 6-27 Psalm 99 Luke 21. 20-28	Collect & PC 140 & 141 Daniel 7. 1-14 Psalm 93 Luke 21. 29-33	Collect & PC 315 & 110 Daniel 7. 15-27 Psalm 95. 1-7 Luke 21. 34-36
Morning Prayer		
Psalm 125; [126; 127; 128] Isaiah 21. 1-12 Matthew 10.34 – 11.1	Psalm 139 Isaiah 22. 1-14 Matthew 11. 2-19	Psalm 145 Isaiah 24 Matthew 11. 20-end
Evening Prayer		
Psalm [131; 132;] 133 Isaiah 41. 8-20 Revelation 16. 12-end	Psalm 146; [147] Isaiah 41.21 – 42.9 Revelation 17	Psalm [148; 149;] 150 Isaiah 42. 10-17 Revelation 18

Alternative Readings

Pages 16 and 17: If the Epiphany is moved to Sunday 5 January use these readings on Monday 6 January.

DAILY EUCHARIST	Morning Prayer	Evening Prayer
Collect & PC 15 & 16	Psalm [8;] 48	Psalm [96;] 97
1 John 3. 11-18	Isaiah 62	Ruth 4. 1-17
Psalm 100	John 2. 13-end	Colossians 4. 2-end
John 1. 43-51		

Advent 2024 - Kingdom 2025

If All Saints is moved to Sunday 2 November 2025 (replacing the First Sunday of The Kingdom) then the following readings should be used on 1st 2nd and 3rd November (See pages 103 and 104).

Saturday 1 November	* ALL SAINTS Sunday 2 November *(replacing Kingdom One)*	All Souls Monday 3 November *(moved from 2 November)*
DAILY EUCHARIST	**PRINCIPAL SERVICE**	**DAILY EUCHARIST**
Collect & PC 126 & 127	Collect & PC 128 & 129	Collect & PC 293 & 389
Romans 11. 1-6, 11, 12, 25-29	Daniel 7. 1-3, 15-18 Psalm 149	Lamentations 3. 17-26 *or* Wisdom 3. 1-9
Psalm 94. 14-19	Ephesians 1. 11-23	Psalm 23 *or* 27. 1-5, 13, 14
Luke 14. 7-11	Luke 6. 20-31	Romans 5. 5-11 *or* 1 Peter 1. 3-9
		John 5. 19-25 *or* John 6. 37-40
Morning Prayer	**THIRD SERVICE**	**Morning Prayer**
Psalm [120;] 121; [122]	Psalm 15; 84	Psalm 31
1 Maccabees 13. 41-end; 14. 4-15 *or* 2 Chronicles 32. 1-22	Isaiah 35. 1-9 Luke 9. 18-27	Judith 15. 1-13 *or* Leviticus 25. 1-24
John 14.15–end		Titus 3
Evening Prayer	**SECOND SERVICE**	**Evening Prayer**
Psalm 118	Psalm 148; 150	Psalm 35
2 Kings 20	Isaiah 65. 17-25	Sirach 51. 1-12
Philippians 4.2–end	Hebrews 11.32 – 12.2	*or* Ecclesiastes 11. 1-8
		John 20.11–18
Evening prayer on the eve of All Saints: Psalm 1; 5 Sirach 44. 1-15 *or* Isaiah 40. 27-31 Revelation 19. 6-10		

Replaced Readings

The following readings have been replaced by a Holy Day.

The readings can be used before *or* after the Holy Day to continue the sequence.

Saturday 25 January *See page 21* (The Conversion of Paul)	Saturday 1 March *See page 31* (David)	Wednesday 19 March *See page 36* (Joseph of Nazareth)
DAILY EUCHARIST		
Collect & PC 21 & 22	Collect & PC 35 & 36	Collect & PC 44 & 45
Hebrews 9. 2-3, 11-14	Sirach 17. 1-15	Jeremiah 18. 18-20
Psalm 47. 1-8	Psalm 103. 1-4, 13-18	Psalm 31. 1-5, 13-16
Mark 3. 20-21	Mark 10. 13-16	Matthew 20. 17-28
Morning Prayer		
Psalm 122; [128; 150]	Psalm 76; [79]	Psalm 35
Hosea 2. 2-17	Eccles. 11.9 – *end of* 12	Jeremiah 8.18 – 9.11
1 Corinthians 9. 1-14	John 20.19–end	John 6. 60-end
Evening Prayer		
Psalm 61; [66]	Psalm [81;] 84	Psalm 3; [51]
Genesis 11. 1-9	Genesis 35	Genesis 44. 18-end
Matthew 25. 31-end	Philemon	Hebrews 2. 10-end

Replaced Readings

Tuesday 25 March *See page 38* (The Annunciation)	Monday 28 April *(moved from 25 April)* *See page 50* (Mark)	Thursday 1 May *See page 51* (Philip and James)
DAILY EUCHARIST		
Collect & PC 46 & 47	Collect & PC 63 & 64	Collect & PC 63 & 64
Song of Three 1. 2, 11-20	Acts 4. 23-13	Acts 5. 27-33
Psalm 25. 4-10	Psalm 2	Psalm 34. 15-22
Matthew 18. 21-35	John 3. 1-8	John 3. 31-36
Morning Prayer		
Psalm [6;] 9	Psalm [2;] 19	Psalm 28; [29]
Jeremiah 11.18 – 12.6	Deuteronomy 1. 3-18	Deuteronomy 4. 1-14
John 7.53 – 8.11	John 20. 1-10	John 21. 1-14
Evening Prayer		
Psalm [61; 62;] 64	Psalm 139	Psalm 34
Genesis 47.28 – *end of* 48	Exodus 15. 1-21	Exodus 17
Hebrews 5.11 – 6.12	Colossians 1. 1-14	Colossians 2.16 – 3.11

Wednesday 14 May *See page 54* (Matthias)	Saturday 31 May *See page 59* (The Visit of the Virgin Mary to Elizabeth)	Wednesday 11 June *See page 62* (Barnabas)
DAILY EUCHARIST		
Collect & PC 67 & 68	Collect & PC 71 & 72	Collect & PC 79 & 80
Acts 12, 24 – 13. 5a	Acts 18. 23-26	2 Corinthians 3. 4-11
Psalm 67	Psalm 47. 1, 2, 6-11	Psalm 99
John 12. 44-50	John 16. 23b-28	Matthew 5. 17-19
Morning Prayer		
Psalm 135	Psalm [21;] 47	Psalm 119. 153-end
Deuteronomy 10. 12-end	Deuteronomy 30	Job 3
Ephesians 5. 1-14	1 John 2. 7-17	Romans 2. 1-16
Evening Prayer		
Psalm 47; [48]	Psalm [84;] 85	Psalm 136
Exodus 33	Numbers 21. 4-9	Joshua 3
Luke 3. 15-22	Luke 7. 18-35	Luke 9. 37-50

Advent 2023 - Kingdom 2024

Thursday 19 June *See page 65* (Holy Communion)	Tueday 24 June *See page 66* (John the Baptist)	Thursday 3 July *See page 69* (Thomas)
DAILY EUCHARIST		
Collect & PC 81 & 82	Collect & PC 83 & 84	Collect & PC 85 & 86
2 Corinthians 11. 1-11	Genesis 13. 2, 5-18	Genesis 22. 1-14
Psalm 111	Psalm 15	Psalm 116. 1-9
Matthew 6. 7-15	Matthew 7. 6, 12-14	Matthew 9. 1-8
Morning Prayer		
Psalm [14;] 15 [; 16]	Psalm [32;] 36	Psalm [56;] 57; [63]
Job 10	Job 14	Job 23
Romans 5. 12-end	Romans 7. 7-end	Romans 10. 11-end
Evening Prayer		
Psalm 18	Psalm 33	Psalm [61;] 62; [64]
Joshua 8. 30-end	Joshua 21.43 – 22.8	Judges 6. 1-24
Luke 11. 14-28	Luke 12. 13-21	Luke 14. 1-11

Tuesday 22 July *See page 74* (Mary Magdalene)	Friday 25 July *See page 75* (James)	Wednesday 6 August *See page 78* (Transfiguration)
DAILY EUCHARIST		
Collect & PC 91 & 92	Collect & PC 91 & 92	Collect & PC 95 & 96
Exodus 14.21 – 15.1	Exodus 20. 1-17	Numbers 13. 1, 2, 25 – 14. 1, 26-35
Psalm 114	Psalm 19. 7-10	Psalm 106. 6-14, 21-23
Matthew 12. 46-50	Matthew 13. 18-23	Matthew 15. 21-28
Morning Prayer		
Psalm [103;] 106	Psalm 139	Psalm 119. 1-32
Ezekiel 1.15 – 2.2	Ezekiel 8	Ezekiel 18. 21-32
2 Corinthians 1.15 – 2.4	2 Corinthians 4	2 Corinthians 12
Evening Prayer		
Psalm 107	Psalm 130; [131; 137]	Psalm 11; [12; 13]
1 Samuel 1.21 – 2.11	1 Samuel 3.1 – 4.1a	1 Samuel 11
Luke 19. 41-end	Luke 20. 20-26	Luke 22. 39-46

Replaced Readings

Friday 15 August *See page 81* (Mary)	Monday 29 September *See page 94* (Michael and All Angels)	Saturday 18 October *See page 99* (Luke)
DAILY EUCHARIST		
Collect & PC 97 & 98	Collect & PC 111 & 112	Collect & PC 115 & 116
Joshua 24. 1-13	Zechariah 8. 1-8	Romans 4. 13-18
Psalm 136. 1-3, 15-21	Psalm 102. 11-22	Psalm 105. 5-10, 42-45
Matthew 19. 3-12	Luke 9. 46-50	Luke 12. 8-12
Morning Prayer		
Psalm 31	Psalm [27;] 30	Psalm 76; [79]
Ezekiel 34. 17-end	Wisdom 6. 12-23 *or* 1 Chronicles 28. 1-10	1 Maccabees 2. 49-end *or* 2 Chronicles 15. 1-15
James 4.13 – 5.6	Mark 11. 1-11	Mark 14. 66-end
Evening Prayer		
Psalm 35	Psalm [26;] 28; [29]	Psalm [81;] 84
1 Samuel 17. 31-54	1 Kings 8. 31-62	2 Kings 4. 1-37
Luke 24. 13-35	Acts 16. 6-24	Acts 25. 13-end

Advent 2023 - Kingdom 2024

Tuesday 28 October *See page 102* (Simon and Jude)	Saturday 1 November *See page 103* (All Saints)	Monday 3 November *See page 104* (All Souls)
DAILY EUCHARIST		
Collect & PC 126 & 127 Romans 8. 18-25 Psalm 126 Luke 13. 18-21	Collect & PC 126 & 127 Romans 11. 1-6, 11, 12, 25-29 Psalm 94. 14-19 Luke 14. 7-11	Collect & PC 131 & 132 Romans 11. 29-36 Psalm 69. 29-36 Luke 14. 12-14
Morning Prayer		
Psalm 106; [103] 1 Maccabees 6. 18-47 *or* 2 Chronicles 28 John 13. 12-20	Psalm [120;] 121; [122] 1 Maccabees 13.41-end: 14.4 – 15 *or* 2 Chronicles 32. 1-22 John 14.15–end	Psalm 2; [146] Isaiah 1. 1-20 Matthew 1. 18-end
Evening Prayer		
Psalm 107 2 Kings 18. 1-12 Philippians 1. 12-end	Psalm 11 2 Kings 20 Philippians 4.2–end	Psalm 92; [96; 97] Daniel 1 Revelation 1

Days of Special Prayer

1 December	World AIDS Day
28 December	Day of Prayer for Refugees
18 - 25 January	Week of Prayer for Christian Unity
27 January	Holocaust Memorial Day
Last Sunday in January	World Leprosy Day
Second Sunday in February	Racial Justice Sunday
First Friday in March	Women's World Day of Prayer
The Sunday after Asension Day	Ministry and Calling Sunday
Between Ascension Day and Pentecost	Prayers for the gifts of the Holy Spirit.
Trinity One	Covenant Sunday
Second week in May	Christian Aid week
Sunday nearest 26 May	Anglican Communion Sunday
5 June	World Environment Day
20 June	World Refugee Day
Second Sunday in July	Sea Sunday
Second Sunday in September	Education Sunday
Sunday nearest 10 October	Homelessness Sunday
Second Sunday in October and the week	Prisoners' Sunday and week
Sunday nearest to 11 November	Remembrance Sunday
Third Sunday in November	Safeguarding Sunday

Fair Trade fortnight: At the time of press no confirmation had been received about the dates.

LECTIONARY BOOK TWO:

Holy Days and other services

Holy Days

		For the colour of the season, see the main Lectionary pages	
29 November	**Vigil and Day of Intercession for the Mission of the Church** (For use at the Eucharist or a non-Eucharistic service) **Collect & PC 314 & 363** Isaiah 49. 1-6 Psalm 96. 1-10 Ephesians 2. 13-18 Matthew 9. 35-38	**Purple** *or* colour of the Season	IV
30 November	**Andrew, Apostle. Patron Saint *of* Scotland** *See Lectionary*	**RED**	II
1 December	**Nicholas Ferrar (1637), Deacon and Founder *of* the Little Gidding Community** **Collect & PC 316 & 383 / 389** Jeremiah 17. 7-10 Psalm 119. 57-64 1 John 2. 12-17 Matthew 19. 23-30 *or* Luke 12. 32-34	Colour of the Season *or* White	V
2 December	**The Saints, Martyrs and Missionaries *of* Asia** **Collect & PC 317 & 365** Isaiah 52. 7-10 *or* Ezekiel 3. 16-21 Psalm 16 *or* 117 *or* 96. 1-4, 10-13 Acts 13, 46-49 *or* Acts 26. 19-23 Matthew 25. 31-46 *or* Luke 5. 1-11	Colour of the Season *or* Red	V
3 December	**Francis Xavier (1552), Missionary *of* Asia** **Collect & PC 318 & 365** Isaiah 52. 7-10 *or* Ezekiel 3. 16-21 Psalm 16 *or* 117 *or* 96. 1-4, 10-13 Acts 13, 46-49 *or* Acts 26. 19-23 Matthew 25. 31-46 *or* Luke 5. 1-11	Colour of the Season *or* White	V
6 December	**Nicholas (c342), Bishop *of* Myra** **Collect & PC 319 & 377 / 379** Isaiah 61. 1-3 Psalm 28. 6-9 1 Timothy 6. 6-11 Mark 10. 13-16	Colour of the Season *or* White	V

7 December	**Ambrose (397), Bishop of Milan and Doctor of the Faith** Collect & PC 320 & 387 Isaiah 41. 9b-13 Psalm 34. 11-18 1 Corinthians 2. 6-13 Luke 22. 24-30	White	or colour of the Season	IV
8 December	**Cynidr (6th century), Bishop *of* Glasbury** Collect & PC 321 & 377 / 379 Ezekiel 34. 11-16 Psalm 28. 6-9 1 Peter 5. 1-4 *or* Ephesians 4. 7, 8, 11-16 John 21. 15-17	Colour of the Season	or White	V
13 December	**Lucy (304), Martyr *in* Syracuse** Collect & PC 322 & 385 Wisdom 3. 1-7 Psalm 28. 6-9 2 Corinthians 4. 6-15 Matthew 10. 24-32 *or* John 15.18 – 16.4a	Colour of the Season	or Red	V
14 December	**John of the Cross (1591), Priest, Poet and Teacher of the Faith** Collect & PC 323 & 356 / 387 Sirach 51. 1-8 Psalm 28. 6-9 Romans 8. 35-39 *or* Revelation 7. 13-17 Matthew 10. 28-33	White	or colour of the Season	IV
17-23 December	**17 - O Wisdom! Collect 324** **18 - O Adonai! Collect 325** **19 - O Root of Jesse! Collect 326** **20 - O Key of David! Collect 327** **21 - O Dayspring! Collect 328** **22 - O King of the Nations! Collect 329** **23 - O Emmanuel! Collect 330** and PC prayer for the week plus the Daily Eucharist *see Lectionary*	Purple		V
25 December	**THE NATIVITY OF OUR LORD** *See Lectionary*	WHITE		I

Holy Days

Date	Commemoration	Colour	
26 December	**Stephen, Deacon and First Martyr** *See Lectionary*	**RED**	II
27 December	**John, Apostle and Evangelist** *See Lectionary*	**WHITE**	II
28 December	**The Holy Innocents** *See Lectionary*	**RED**	II
29 December	**Thomas Becket (1170), Archbishop *of* Canterbury and Martyr** **Collect & PC 334 & 385** Isaiah 61. 1-3 Psalm 28. 6-9 1 Timothy 6. 6-11 Mark 10. 13-16	**Red** *or* colour of the Season	IV
30 December	**Tathan (6th century), Welsh Abbot and Teacher of the Faith** **Collect & PC 335 & 383** Jeremiah 17. 7-10 Psalm 119. 57-64 1 John 2. 12-17 Matthew 19. 23-30 *or* Luke 12. 32-34	**Colour of the Season** *or* White	V
31 December	**John Wycliffe (1384), Priest, Reformer and Translator of the Scriptures** **Collect & PC 336 & 392** *either* / *or* Isaiah 52. 7-10 / Ezekiel 34. 11-16 Psalm 106. 1-4, 19-23 / Psalm 23 1 Corinthians 4. 1-5 / 1 Peter 5. 1-4 Matthew 23. 8-12 / John 10. 11-16	**Colour of the Season** *or* White	V
1 January	**NAMING OF JESUS** *See Lectionary*	**WHITE**	I
3 January	**Morris Williams [bardic name 'Nicander'](1874), Welsh Priest and Poet** **Collect & PC 143 & 375** Song of Solomon 2. 8-14 Psalm 5. 1-8 Revelation 19. 11-16 John 17. 20-26	**Colour of the Season** *or* White	V

6 January	**THE EPIPHANY OF OUR LORD** *See Lectionary*	**WHITE**	I
10 January	**William Laud (1645), Archbishop *of* Canterbury** **Collect & PC 144 & 379** Ezekiel 34. 11-16 Psalm 28. 6-9 1 Peter 5. 1-4 *or* Ephesians 4. 7, 8, 11-16 John 21. 15-17	**Colour of the Season** *or* White	V
11 January	**Rhys Prichard (1644), Priest,** **William Williams (1791), Deacon** **and Isaac Williams (1865), Priest; Poets** **Collect & PC 145 & 375** Song of Solomon 2. 8-14 Psalm 5. 1-8 Revelation 19. 11-16 John 17. 20-26	**Colour of the Season** *or* White	V
13 January	**Hilary (368),** **Bishop *of* Poitiers and Teacher of the Faith** **Collect & PC 146 & 379** Ezekiel 34. 11-16 Psalm 28. 6-9 1 John 2. 18-25 John 8. 25-32	White *or* colour of the Season	IV
14 January	**Kentigern (c603),** **Missionary and Bishop *of* Strathclyde** **Collect & PC 147 & 379** Ezekiel 34. 11-16 Psalm 28. 6-9 1 Peter 5. 1-4 *or* Ephesians 4. 7, 8, 11-16 John 21. 15-17	White *or* colour of the Season	IV
17 January	**Antony *of* Egypt (356), Hermit and Abbot** **Collect & PC 148 & 383** Jeremiah 17. 7-10 Psalm 119. 57-64 Philippians 3. 7-14 Matthew 19. 16-26	White *or* colour of the Season	IV

Holy Days

Date	Commemoration	Colour	
18 January	**The Confession of Peter, Apostle** **Collect & PC 149 & 110** Acts 4. 8-13 *or* 1 Peter 5. 1-4 Psalm 23 Matthew 16. 13-19	White *or* colour of the Season	IV
21 January	**Agnes (304), Child Martyr *in* Rome** **Collect & PC 150 & 385** Wisdom 3. 1-9 Psalm 28. 6-9 Revelation 7. 13-17 Matthew 10. 24-32 *or* John 15.18 - 16.4a	Colour of the Season *or* Red	V
24 January	**Francis de Sales (1622),** **Bishop *of* Geneva and Teacher of the Faith** **Collect & PC 151 & 379** Proverbs 3. 13-18 Psalm 28. 6-9 1 Peter 5. 1-4 *or* Ephesians 4. 7, 8, 11-16 John 3. 17-21	Colour of the Season *or* White	V
25 January	**The Conversion of Paul, Apostle** *See Lectionary*	WHITE	II
26 January	**Timothy *and* Titus, Companions of Paul** **Collect & PC 154 & 363 / 365** Isaiah 61. 1-3a Psalm 100 2 Timothy 1. 1-8 *or* Titus 1. 1-5 Luke 10. 1-9	White *or* colour of the Season	IV
27 January	**John Chrysostom (407),** **Bishop *of* Constantinople and Doctor of the Faith** **Collect & PC 155 & 356 / 387** Jeremiah 1. 4-10 Psalm 34. 11-18 1 Corinthians 2. 6-13 Matthew 5. 13-19	White *or* colour of the Season	IV
28 January	**Thomas Aquinas (1274), Teacher of the Faith** **Collect & PC 156 & 356 / 387** Wisdom 7. 7-10, 15, 16 Psalm 34. 11-18 1 Corinthians 2. 9-16 John 16. 12-15	White *or* colour of the Season	IV

Holy Days

Date	Commemoration	Colour	
1 February	**Brigid *or* Bride (c525), Abbess *of* Kildare** Collect & PC 157 & 383 Jeremiah 17. 7-10 Psalm 119. 57-64 1 John 2. 12-17 Matthew 19. 23-30 *or* Luke 12. 32-34	Colour of the Season *or* White	V
2 February	**THE PRESENTATION OF CHRIST (Candlemas)** *See Lectionary*	WHITE	I
3 February	**The Saints, Martyrs *and* Missionaries *of* Europe** Collect & PC 158 & 365 Isaiah 52. 7-10 *or* Ezekiel 3. 16-21 Psalm 16 *or* Psalm 96. 1-4, 10-13 *or* Psalm 117 Acts 13. 46-49 *or* Acts 26. 19-23 Matthew 25. 31-46 *or* Luke 5. 1-11	Colour of the Season *or* Red	V
	Seiriol (6th century), Welsh Abbot Collect & PC 159 & 383 Jeremiah 17. 7-10 Psalm 119. 57-64 1 John 2. 12-17 Matthew 19. 23-30 *or* Luke 12. 32-34	Colour of the Season *or* White	V
4 February	**Manche Masemola (1928), Child Martyr *in* South Africa** Collect & PC 160 & 385 Wisdom 3. 1-9 Psalm 28. 6-9 Romans 8. 35-39 *or* Revelation 7. 13-17 Matthew 10. 24-32 *or* John 15.18 – 16.4a	Colour of the Season *or* Red	V
9 February	**Teilo (6th century), Bishop *of* Llandaff** Collect & PC 161 & 379 Ezekiel 34. 11-16 Psalm 28. 6-9 1 Peter 5. 1-4 *or* Ephesians 4. 7, 8, 11-16 John 21. 15-17	White *or* colour of the Season	IV
14 February	**Cyril (869), Monk *and* Methodius (885), Bishop; Translators of Scripture and Missionaries** Collect & PC 162 & 365 Isaiah 52. 7-10 Psalm 117 *or* 96. 1-4, 10-13 Romans 10. 11-15 Matthew 25. 31-46 *or* Luke 5. 1-11	Colour of the Season *or* White	V

Holy Days

Date	Commemoration	Colour	
18 February	**John of Fiesole [Fra Angelico](1455), Priest *and* Andrei Rublev (c1430), Monk; Painters** **Collect & PC 163 & 389** Song of Solomon 2. 8-14 Psalm 5. 1-8 Revelation 19. 11-16 John 17. 20-26	Colour of the Season *or* White	V
19 February	**Thomas Burgess (1837), Bishop *of* St Davids and Teacher of the Faith** **Collect & PC 164 & 356 / 387** Sirach 39. 1-9 Psalm 34. 11-18 1 Corinthians 2. 6-13 Matthew 13. 51-52	Colour of the Season *or* White	V
20 February	**The Saints, Martyrs and Missionaries *of* Africa** **Collect & PC 165 & 365** Isaiah 52. 7-10 *or* Ezekiel 3. 16-21 Psalm 16 *or* Psalm 96. 1-4, 10-13 *or* Psalm 117 Acts 13. 46-49 *or* Acts 26. 19-23 Matthew 25. 31-46 *or* Luke 5. 1-11	Colour of the Season *or* Red	V
23 February	**Polycarp (c155), Bishop *of* Smyrna and Martyr** **Collect & PC 166 & 385** Wisdom 3. 1-9 Psalm 28. 6-9 Revelation 2. 8-11 Matthew 10. 24-32 *or* John 15.18 – 16.4a	Red *or* colour of the Season	IV
27 February	**George Herbert (1633), Priest *and* all Pastors** **Collect & PC 167 & 381** *either* / *or* Malachi 2. 5-7 / Ezekiel 34. 11-16 Psalm 106. 1-4, 19-23 / Psalm 23 Revelation 19. 5-9 / Peter 5. 1-4 Matthew 11. 25-30 / John 10. 11-16	Colour of the Season *or* White	V
1 March	**David (6th century), Bishop *of* St Davids and Patron *of* Wales** *See Lectionary*	WHITE	II

Holy Days

2 March	Chad (672), Bishop *of* Mercia and Missionary **Collect & PC 199 & 379** John 17. 20-26 Ezekiel 34. 11-16 Psalm 28. 6-9 1 Timothy 6. 11b-16 John 21. 15-17	White *or* colour of the Season	IV
5 March	Non (5th century), Mother of David *of* Wales **Collect & PC 170 & 391** Malachi 3. 16-18 Psalm 145. 3-13a Revelation 19. 5-8 John 17. 18-23	Colour of the Season *or* White	V
7 March	Perpetua, Felicity *and* their Companions (203), Martyrs in Carthage **Collect & PC 171 & 385** Wisdom 3. 1-9 Psalm 28. 6-9 Revelation 12. 10-12a Matthew 10. 24-32 *or* John 15.18 – 16.4a	Red *or* colour of the Season	IV
17 March	Patrick (5th century), Bishop, Missionary and Patron *of* Ireland **Collect & PC 172 & 365** Isaiah 51. 1-8 Psalm 91. 1-4, 13-16 Acts 16. 6-15 Luke 10. 1-12, 17-20	White *or* colour of the Season	IV
18 March	Cyril of Jerusalem (386), Bishop and Teacher of the Faith **Collect & PC 173 & 379** Ezekiel 34. 11-16 Psalm 28. 6-9 1 Peter 5. 1-4 *or* Ephesians 4. 7-8, 11-16 John 21. 15-17	Colour of the Season *or* White	V
19 March	Joseph *of* Nazareth *See Lectionary*	**WHITE**	II

Holy Days

20 March	**Cuthbert (687),** **Bishop *of* Lindisfarne and Missionary** **Collect & PC 260 & 378 / 379** Ezekiel 34. 11-16 Psalm 28. 6-9 1 Peter 5. 1-4 *or* Ephesians 4. 7, 8, 11-16 Matthew 18. 12-14	White *or* colour of the Season	IV
21 March	**Thomas Cranmer (1566), Hugh Latimer, Nicholas Ridley and Robert Ferrar (1555), Bishops, Teachers of the Faith and Reformation era Martyrs** **Collect & PC 175 & 291** Isaiah 43. 1-7 *or* Sirach 2. 10-18 Psalm 87 2 Corinthians 4. 5-12 John 12. 20-26	Colour of the Season *or* Red	V
24 March	**Oscar Romero (1980),** **Bishop *of* San Salvador and Martyr** **Collect & PC 176 & 385** Isaiah 58. 6-11 Psalm 146. 5-10 1 John 3. 14-18 Matthew 25. 31-46	Colour of the Season *or* Red	V
25 March	**The Annunciation of Our Lord to the Blessed Virgin Mary** *See Lectionary*	WHITE	II
29 March	**Woolos, (6th century), Welsh King** **Collect & PC 178 & 391** 1 Samuel 16. 1-13a Psalm 72. 1-7 1 Timothy 2. 1-6 Mark 10. 42-45	White *or* colour of the Season	IV
7 April	**Brynach (5th Century), Welsh Abbot** **Collect & PC 179 & 383** Jeremiah 17. 7-10 Psalm 119. 57-64 1 John 2. 12-17 Matthew 19. 23-30 *or* Luke 12. 32-34	Colour of the Season *or* White	V

Holy Days

Date	Commemoration	Colour	
8 April	**Griffith Jones (1761), Priest and Teacher of the Faith** **Collect & PC 180 & 377** *either* Isaiah 52. 7-10 Psalm 106. 1-4, 19-23 1 Corinthians 4. 1-5 Matthew 23. 8-12 *or* Ezekiel 34. 11-16 Psalm 23 1 Peter 5. 1-4 John 10. 11-16	Colour of the Season *or* White	V
9 April	**Saints, Martyrs *and* Missionaries *of* South America** **Collect & PC 181 & 365** Isaiah 52. 7-10 *or* Ezekiel 3. 16-21 Psalm 16 *or* 117 *or* 96. 1-4, 10-13 Acts 13. 46-49 *or* Acts 26. 19-23 Matthew 25. 31-46 *or* Luke 5. 1-11	Colour of the Season *or* Red	V
	Dietrich Bonhoeffer (1945), Lutheran Pastor, Teacher of the Faith and Martyr *in* Flossenbürg **Collect & PC 182 & 385** Wisdom 3. 1-9 Psalm 28. 6-9 Romans 8. 35-39 *or* Revelation 7. 13-17 Matthew 10. 24-32 *or* John 15.18 – 16.4a	Colour of the Season *or* Red	V
11 April	**George Augustus Selwyn (1878), first Bishop *of* New Zealand and Missionary** **Collect & PC 183 & 365** Isaiah 52. 7-10 *or* Ezekiel 3. 16-21 Psalm 16 *or* Psalm 96. 1-4, 10-13 *or* Psalm 117 Acts 13. 46-49 *or* Acts 26. 19-23 Matthew 25. 31-46 *or* Luke 5. 1-11	Colour of the Season *or* White	V
15 April	**Padarn (6th century), Welsh Bishop** **Collect & PC 184 & 379** Ezekiel 34. 11-16 Psalm 28. 6-9 1 Peter 5. 1-4 *or* Ephesians 4. 7, 8, 11-16 John 21. 15-17	White *or* colour of the Season	IV
20 April	**Beuno (c640), Welsh Abbot** **Collect & PC 185 & 383** Jeremiah 17. 7-10 Psalm 119. 57-64 1 John 2. 12-17 Matthew 19. 23-30 *or* Luke 12. 32-34	White *or* colour of the Season	IV

Holy Days

Date	Commemoration	Colour	Rank
21 April	**Anselm (1109), Archbishop of Canterbury and Teacher of the Faith** **Collect & PC 186 & 387** Wisdom 9. 13-18 Psalm 34. 11-18 Romans 5. 8-11 Matthew 13. 51, 52	White *or* colour of the Season	IV
23 April	**George (304), Martyr and Patron of England** **Collect & PC 187 & 389** 1 Maccabees 2. 59-64 *or* Revelation 12. 7-12 Psalm 126 2 Timothy 2. 3-13 John 15.18-21	Red *or* colour of the Season	IV
25 April	**Mark, Evangelist** *See Lectionary*	RED	II
29 April	**Catherine of Siena (1380), Writer and Teacher of the Faith** **Collect & PC 189 & 375 / 389** Proverbs 8.1, 6-11 Psalm 15 Philippians 4. 4-9 John 17. 12-26	White *or* colour of the Season	IV
1 May	**Philip and James, Apostles** *See Lectionary*	RED	II
2 May	**Athanasius (373), Bishop of Alexandria and Teacher of the Faith** **Collect & PC 191 & 356 / 387** Sirach 4. 20-28 Psalm 34. 11-18 1 Corinthians 2. 6-13 Matthew 10. 24-27	White *or* colour of the Season	IV
3 May	**Henry Vaughan (1695), Welsh Poet** **Collect & PC 192 & 375** Song of Solomon 2. 8-14 Psalm 5. 1-8 Revelation 19. 11-16 John 17. 20-26	Colour of the Season *or* White	V

Holy Days

Date	Commemoration	Colour	
5 May	**Asaph (6th century), Bishop of St Asaph** **Collect & PC 193 & 379** Ezekiel 34. 11-16 Psalm 28. 6-9 1 Peter 5. 1-4 *or* Ephesians 4. 7, 8, 11-16 John 21. 15-17	Colour of the Season *or* White	V
8 May	**Julian of Norwich (c1417), Spiritual Writer** **Collect & PC 194 & 389** Sirach 2. 1-9 Psalm 15 1 Corinthians 13. 8-13 Matthew 5. 13-19	Colour of the Season *or* White	V
9 May	**Gregory of Nazianzus (390),** **Bishop and Doctor of the Faith** **Collect & PC 195 & 379** Ezekiel 34. 11-16 Psalm 28. 6-9 2 Timothy 4. 1-8 Matthew 5. 13-19	Colour of the Season *or* White	V
14 May	**Matthias, Apostle.** *See Lectionary*	**RED**	II
15 May	**Edmwnd Prys (1624), Priest and Poet** ***and* John Davies (1644), Priest; Translators** **Collect & PC 197 & 392** *either* *or* Deuteronomy 6. 3-9 1 Kings 19. 16,19-21 Psalm 16 Psalm 128 Ephesians 4. 1-7, 11-13 2 Corinthians 5. 14-20 Matthew 25. 14-30 John 15. 9-17	Colour of the Season *or* White	V
19 May	**Dunstan (988), Archbishop of Canterbury** **Collect & PC 198 & 379** Exodus 31. 1-5 Psalm 28. 6-9 1 Peter 5. 1-4 *or* Ephesians 4. 7, 8, 11-16 Matthew 24. 42-46	Colour of the Season *or* White	V

Holy Days

24 May	**Charles Wesley (1788) and John Wesley (1791), Hymn Writers, Priests and Missionaries** **Collect & PC 200 & 365** Isaiah 52. 7-10 *or* Ezekiel 3. 16-21 Psalm 16 *or* Psalm 96. 1-4, 10-13 *or* Psalm 117 Ephesians 5. 15-20 Matthew 25, 31-46 *or* Luke 5. 1-11	Colour of the Season *or* White	V
25 May	**Bede (735), Teacher of the Faith and Writer** **Collect & PC 201 & 356 / 387** Sirach 39. 1-10 Psalm 34. 11-18 1 Corinthians 2. 6-13 Matthew 13. 51, 52	White *or* colour of the Season	IV
26 May	**Augustine (605), First Archbishop *of* Canterbury** **Collect & PC 202 & 377 / 379** Ezekiel 34. 11-16 Psalm 28. 6-9 1 Thessalonians 2. 2b-8 Matthew 13. 31-33	White *or* colour of the Season	IV
28 May	**Melangell (6th century), Welsh Abbess** **Collect & PC 203 & 383** Jeremiah 17. 7-10 Psalm 119. 57-64 1 John 2. 12-17 Matthew 19. 23-30 *or* Luke 12. 32-34	Colour of the Season *or* White	V
31 May	**The Visit of the Virgin Mary to Elizabeth** *See Lectionary*	**WHITE**	II
1 June	**Justin (c165), Apologist and Martyr *in* Rome** **Collect & PC 205 & 385** 1 Maccabees 2. 15-22 Psalm 28. 6-9 1 Corinthians 1. 18-25 John 15. 18-21	**Red** *or* colour of the Season	IV

Holy Days

2 June	**Blandina *and* her Companions (177), Martyrs in Lyon** **Collect & PC 206 & 385** Wisdom 3. 1-9 Psalm 28. 6-9 Romans 8. 35-39 *or* Revelation 7. 13-17 Matthew 10. 24-32 *or* John 15.18 – 16.4a	Red *or* colour of the Season	IV
3 June	**James Hannington (1885), Bishop, Missionary and Martyr, the Martyrs *of* Uganda (1886) *and* Janani Luwum (1977), Bishop and Martyr** **Collect & PC 207 & 385** *either* *or* Sirach 4.20-28 Genesis 14. 18-20 Psalm 28. 6-9 Psalm 116. 12-19 Romans 8. 35-39 1 Corinthians 11. *or* Revelation 7. 13-17 23-26, [27-29, 31-34a] Matthew 10. 24-32 John 6. [47-50,] 51-58 *or* John 12. 24-32	Colour of the Season *or* Red	V
5 June	**Boniface (754), Archbishop *of* Mainz, Missionary and Martyr** **Collect & PC 208 & 385** Wisdom 3. 1-9 Psalm 28. 6-9 Acts 20. 24-28 Matthew 10. 24-32 *or* John 15.18-16.4a	Colour of the Season *or* Red	V
9 June	**Columba (597), Abbot *of* Iona and Missionary** **Collect & PC 209 & 383** Jeremiah 17. 7-10 Psalm 119. 57-64 Titus 2. 11-15 Matthew 19. 23-30 *or* Luke 12. 32-34	White *or* colour of the Season	IV
10 June	**Ephrem *of* Syria (373), Deacon, Hymn Writer and Teacher of the Faith** **Collect & PC 210 & 375** Sirach 39. 1-9 Psalm 34. 11-18 1 Corinthians 2. 6-13 Matthew 13. 51, 52	Colour of the Season *or* White	V
11 June	**Barnabas, Apostles.** *See Lectionary*	RED	II

Holy Days

14 June	**Basil the Great (397), Bishop and Doctor of the Faith** **Collect & PC 212 & 356 / 387** Sirach 39. 1-9 Psalm 34. 11-18 2 Timothy 4. 1-8 Matthew 5. 13-19	Colour of the Season *or* White	V
16 June	**Richard (1253), Bishop *of* Chichester** **Collect & PC 212 & 356 / 387** Ezekiel 34. 11-16 Psalm 28. 6-9 1 Peter 5. 1-4 *or* Ephesians 4. 7, 8, 11-16 John 21. 15-19	Colour of the Season *or* White	V
20 June	**Alban (250), Julius *and* Aaron (304-5), Martyrs *from* Roman Britain** **Collect & PC 214 & 385** Wisdom 3. 1-9 Psalm 28. 6-9 2 Timothy 2. 3-13 John 12. 24-26	**Red** *or* colour of the Season	IV
24 June	**The Nativity of John the Baptist** *See Lectionary*	**WHITE**	II
28 June	**Irenæus (c200), Bishop of Lyon and Teacher of the Faith** **Collect & PC 216 & 356 / 387** Sirach 39. 1-9 Psalm 34. 11-18 2 Peter 1. 16-21 Matthew 13. 51, 52	White *or* colour of the Season	IV
28 June	*Evening Prayer on the eve of:* **Peter** Psalm 66; 67 Ezekiel 34. 1-11 Acts 9. 32-43 **Peter *and* Paul** Psalm 66; 67 Ezekiel 3. 4-11 Galatians 1.13 – 2.8		

Holy Days

29 June	**Peter, Apostle** *or* **Peter** *and* **Paul, Apostles** **Collect & PC** (Peter) 217 & 110 **Collect & PC** (Peter and Paul) 218 & 110 **Peter**	**Peter** *and* **Paul** Ezekiel 3. 22-27	Zechariah 4. 1-6a, 10b-14	**RED**	**II**

29 June	**Peter, Apostle** *or* **Peter** *and* **Paul, Apostles** **Collect & PC** (Peter) 217 & 110 **Collect & PC** (Peter and Paul) 218 & 110 **Peter** Ezekiel 3. 22-27 Psalm 125 Acts 12. 1-11 Matthew 16. 13-19 *or* Acts 12. 1-11 Psalm 125 1 Peter 2. 19-25 Matthew 16. 13-19 **Peter, Apostle** *or* **Peter** *and* **Paul, Apostles** **Morning Prayer** Psalm 71 Isaiah 49. 1-6 Acts 11. 1-18	**Peter** *and* **Paul** Zechariah 4. 1-6a, 10b-14 Psalm 125 Acts 12. 1-11 Matthew 16. 13-19 *or* Acts 12. 1-11 Psalm 125 2 Timothy 4. 6-8, 17, 18 Matthew 16. 13-19 **Evening Prayer** Psalm 124; 138 Ezekiel 34. 11-16 John 21. 15-22	**RED**	**II**
30 June	**The Martyrdom of Paul, Apostle** **Collect & PC** 219 & 110 Wisdom 3. 1-9 Psalm 28. 6-9 2 Timothy 4. 6-8 Matthew 10. 24-32 *or* John 15.18 – 16.4a		Red *or* colour of the Season	**IV**
1 July	**Euddogwy (6th century), Bishop** *of* **Llandaff** **Collect & PC** 220 & 379 Ezekiel 34. 11-16 Psalm 28. 6-9 1 Peter 5. 1-4 *or* Ephesians 4. 7, 8, 11-16 John 21.15-17		White *or* colour of the Season	**IV**
3 July	**Thomas, Apostle.** *See Lectionary*		**RED**	**II**

Holy Days

4 July	Peblig (4th century), Welsh Abbot Collect & PC 222 & 383 Jeremiah 17. 7-10 Psalm 119. 57-64 1 John 2. 12-17 Matthew 19. 23-30 *or* Luke 12. 32-34	Colour of the Season *or* White	V
6 July	Thomas More (1535), Martyr of the Reformation Era Collect & PC 223 & 385 Wisdom 3. 1-9 Psalm 28. 6-9 Romans 8. 35-39 *or* Revelation 7. 13-17 Matthew 10. 24-32 *or* John 15.18 – 16.4a	Colour of the Season *or* Red	V
11 July	Benedict of Nursia (c540), Abbott *of* Monte Cassino and Father of Western Monasticism Collect & PC 224 & 383 Jeremiah 17. 7-10 Psalm 119. 57-64 1 Corinthians 3. 10, 11 Luke 18. 18-22	White *or* colour of the Season	IV
14 July	John Keble (1886), Priest, Poet and Teacher of the Faith Collect & PC 225 & 377 Lamentations 3. 19-26 Psalm 34. 11-18 1 Corinthians 2. 6-13 Matthew 5. 1-8	Colour of the Season *or* White	V
18 July	Elizabeth *of* Russia (1918), Religious and Martyr Collect & PC 226 & 385 Isaiah 58. 6-11 Psalm 82 Hebrews 13. 1-3 Matthew 5. 1-12	Colour of the Season *or* Red	V
19 July	Gregory (c394), Bishop *of* Nyssa *and* his sister Macrina (c379), Teachers of the Faith Collect & PC 227 & 387 Wisdom 9. 13-17 Psalm 34. 11-18 1 Corinthians 2. 9-13 Matthew 13. 51, 52	Colour of the Season *or* White	V

Holy Days

Date	Commemoration	Colour	
21 July	**Howell Harris (1773), Welsh Preacher** **Collect & PC 228 & 381** Malachi 3. 16-18 Psalm 145. 3-13a Revelation 19. 5-8 John 17. 18-23	Colour of the Season or White	V
22 July	**Mary Magdalene, follower of Jesus** *See Lectionary*	**WHITE**	II
23 July	**Bridget *of* Sweden (1373), Abbess *of* Vadstena** **Collect 394 & PC 383** Galatians 2. 19-20 Psalm 34. 1-10 John 15. 1-8	Colour of the Season or White	V
25 July	**James, Apostle** *See Lectionary*	**RED**	II
26 July	**Anne *and* Joachim,** **Parents of the Blessed Virgin Mary** **Collect & PC 231 & 389** Zephaniah 3. 14-17 Psalm 127 Romans 8. 28-30 Matthew 13. 16,17	White or colour of the Season	IV
27 July	**Martha, Mary *and* Lazarus *of* Bethany,** **Companions of Our Lord** **Collect & PC 232 & 389** Isaiah 25. 6-9 Psalm 49. 5-10, 16 Hebrews 2. 10-15 John 12. 1-8	White or colour of the Season	IV
28 July	**Samson (5th century), Welsh Bishop** **Collect & PC 233 & 379** Ezekiel 34. 11-16 Psalm 28. 6-9 1 Peter 5. 1-4 *or* Ephesians 4. 7, 8, 11-16 John 21. 15-17	White or colour of the Season	IV

Holy Days

Date	Commemoration	Colour	
29 July	**William Wilberforce (1833), Josephine Butler (1906) *and* all Social Reformers** **Collect & PC 234 & 373** Isaiah 58. 6-11 *or* Job 31. 16-23 Psalm 72. 1-4, 12-14 Galatians 3. 26-29; 4. 6, 7 *or* 1 John 3. 18-23 Matthew 9. 10-13 *or* Luke 4. 16-21	Colour of the Season *or* White	V
30 July	**Silas, Companion of Paul and Missionary** **Collect & PC 235 & 365** Isaiah 52. 7-10 *or* Ezekiel 3. 16-21 Psalm 16 *or* 117 *or* 96. 1-4, 10-13 Acts 13. 46-49 *or* Acts 26, 19-23 Matthew 25. 31-46 *or* Luke 5. 1-11	White *or* colour of the Season	IV
31 July	**Joseph *of* Arimathea** **Collect & PC 236 & 389** Sirach 2. 1-9 Psalm 15 Philippians 4. 4-9 John 19. [31-37,] 38-42	White *or* colour of the Season	IV
	Ignatius *of* Loyola (1556), **Priest and Founder of the Society of Jesus** **Collect & PC 395 & 377** 1 Corinthians 10.31 – 11.1 Psalm 34. 1-10 Luke 14. 25-33	Colour of the Season *or* White	V
3 August	**Germanus (5th century), Bishop *of* Auxerre** **Collect & PC 237 & 379** Ezekiel 34. 11-16 Psalm 28. 6-9 1 Peter 5. 1-4 *or* Ephesians 4. 7, 8, 11-16 John 21. 15-17	White *or* colour of the Season	IV
5 August	**Oswald (642), King *of* Northumbria and Martyr** **Collect & PC 238 & 385** Wisdom 3. 1-9 Psalm 28. 6-9 1 Peter 4. 12-19 John 16. 29-33	Colour of the Season *or* Red	V

6 August	**Transfiguration of Our Lord** *See Lectionary*	**WHITE**	II
8 August	**Dominic (1221),** **Priest and Founder of the Order of Preachers** **Collect & PC 240 & 381** Sirach 39. 1-10 Psalm 119. 57-64 1 John 2. 12-17 Matthew 19. 23-30 *or* Luke 12. 32-34	White *or* colour of the Season	IV
9 August	**Augustine Baker (1641), Priest and Monk** **Collect & PC 241 & 377** *either* — *or* Deuteronomy 6. 3-9 — 1 Kings 19. 16, 19-21 Psalm 16 — Psalm 128 Ephesians 4. 1-7, 11-13 — 2 Corinthians 5. 14-20 Matthew 25. 14-30 — John 15. 9-17	Colour of the Season *or* White	V
	Mary Sumner (1921), **founder of the Mothers' Union** **Collect & PC 242 & 373** Proverbs 31. 10-13, [14-18,] 19, 20, [21-29,] 30, 31 Psalm 127 *and / or* 128 1 Peter 3. 1-9 Mark 3. 31-35 *or* Luke 10. 38-42	Colour of the Season *or* White	V
	Edith Stein (1942), **Teacher of the Faith and Martyr** *in* **Auschwitz** **Collect & PC 243 & 385** Wisdom 3. 1-9 Psalm 28. 6-9 Romans 8. 35-39 *or* Revelation 7. 13-17 Matthew 10. 24-32 *or* John 15.18 – 16.4a	Colour of the Season *or* Red	V
10 August	**Lawrence (258), Deacon** *in* **Rome and Martyr** **Collect & PC 244 & 385** Wisdom 3. 1-9 Psalm 28. 6-9 2 Corinthians 9. 6-10 Matthew 10. 24-32 *or* John 15.18 – 16.4a	Colour of the Season *or* Red	V

Holy Days

Date	Commemoration	Colour	
11 August	**Clare *of* Assisi (1253), Mendicant and founder of the Poor Clares** **Collect & PC 245 & 383** Song of Solomon 8. 6, 7 Psalm 119. 57-64 1 John 2. 12-17 Matthew 19.23-30 *or* Luke 12. 32-34	White *or* colour of the Season	IV
12 August	**Ann Griffiths (1805), Welsh Poet** **Collect & PC 246 & 375** Song of Solomon 2. 8-14 Psalm 5. 1-8 Revelation 19. 11-16 John 17. 20-26	Colour of the Season *or* White	V
13 August	**Jeremy Taylor (1667), Bishop *of* Down and Connor and Teacher of the Faith** **Collect & PC 247 & 379** Ezekiel 34. 11-16 Psalm 28. 6-9 Titus 2. 7, 8, 11-14 John 21. 15-17	Colour of the Season *or* White	V
14 August	**Maximilian Kolbe (1941), Priest and Martyr *in* Auschwitz** **Collect & PC 248 & 385** Wisdom 3. 1-9 Psalm 28. 6-9 Romans 8. 35-39 *or* Revelation 7. 13-17 Matthew 10. 24-32 *or* John 15.18 – 16.4a	Colour of the Season *or* Red	V
15 August	**Mary, Mother of Our Lord** *See Lectionary*	**WHITE**	II
20 August	**Bernard (1153), Abbot *of* Clairvaux and Teacher of the Faith** **Collect & PC 250 & 383** Jeremiah 17. 7-10 Psalm 119. 57-64 Revelation 19. 5-9 Matthew 19, 23-30 *or* Luke 12. 32-34	Colour of the Season *or* White	V

Holy Days

23 August	**Tydfil (430), Welsh Martyr** Collect & PC 251 & 385 Wisdom 3. 1-9 Psalm 28. 6-9 Romans 8. 35-39 *or* Revelation 7. 13-17 Matthew 10. 24-32 *or* John 15.18 – 16.4a	Colour of the Season *or* Red	V
24 August	**Bartholomew, Apostle** *See Lectionary*	**RED**	II
27 August	**Monica (378), Mother of Augustine *of* Hippo** Collect & PC 253 & 389 Sirach 26. 1-3, 13-16 Psalm 127; 128 Philippians 4. 4-9 John 17. 18-23	White *or* colour of the Season	IV
28 August	**Augustine *of* Hippo (430), Bishop and Doctor of the Faith** Collect & PC 254 & 356 / 387 Sirach 39. 1-10 Psalm 34. 11-18 Romans 13. 11-13 Matthew 13. 51, 52	White *or* colour of the Season	IV
29 August	**The Beheading of John the Baptist** Collect & PC 255 & 256 Jeremiah 1. 4-10 Psalm 11 Hebrews 11.32 – 12.2 Matthew 14. 1-12	Red *or* colour of the Season	IV
31 August	**Aidan (651), Bishop *of* Lindisfarne and Missionary** Collect & PC 257 & 379 Ezekiel 34. 11-16 Psalm 28. 6-9 1 Corinthians 9. 16-19 John 21. 15-17	White *or* colour of the Season	IV

Holy Days

Date	Commemoration	Colour	
2 September	**Lucian Tapiedi (1942), Missionary and Martyr** *and* **the Martyrs of Papua New Guinea (1901 & 1942)** Collect & PC 258 & 385 Wisdom 3. 1-9 Psalm 28. 6-9 Romans 8. 35-39 *or* Revelation 7. 13-17 Matthew 10. 24-32 *or* John 15.18 – 16.4a	**Colour of the Season** *or* Red	V
3 September	**Gregory the Great (604),** **Bishop *of* Rome and Doctor of the Faith** Collect & PC 259 & 356 / 387 Sirach 39. 1-9 Psalm 34. 11-18 1 Thessalonians 2. 3-8 Matthew 13. 51, 52	White *or* colour of the Season	IV
8 September	**The Nativity of the Blessed Virgin Mary** Collect & PC 261 & 8 Genesis 3. 8-15 Psalm 45. 6-11, 17 Romans 5. 12-15 Luke 11. 27, 28	White *or* colour of the Season	IV
10 September	**William Salesbury (1584)** *and* **William Morgan (1604), Bishop; Translators** Collect & PC 262 & 392 Malachi 3. 16-18 Psalm 145. 3-13a Revelation 19. 5-8 John 17. 18-23	**Colour of the Season** *or* White	V
11 September	**Deiniol (6th century), Welsh Bishop** Collect & PC 263 & 379 Ezekiel 34. 11-16 Psalm 28. 6-9 1 Peter 5. 1-4 *or* Ephesians 4. 7, 8, 11-16 John 21. 15-17	White *or* colour of the Season	IV
13 September	**Cyprian (258), Bishop *of* Carthage,** **Teacher of the Faith and Martyr** Collect & PC 264 & 385 Wisdom 3. 1-9 Psalm 28. 6-9 1 Peter 4. 12-19 Matthew 18. 18-22	Red *or* colour of the Season	IV

Holy Days

Date	Commemoration	Colour	
14 September	**Holy Cross** *See Lectionary*	**RED**	II
16 September	**Ninian (c430), Bishop *of* Galloway, Apostle of the Picts and Missionary** **Collect & PC 266 & 379** Ezekiel 34. 11-16 Psalm 28. 6-9 Acts 13. 46-49 Mark 16. 15-20	White *or* colour of the Season	IV
20 September	**Saints, Martyrs & Missionaries *of* Australasia and the Pacific** **Collect & PC 267 & 365** Isaiah 52. 7-10 *or* Ezekiel 3. 16-21 Psalm 16 *or* 96. 1-4, 10-13 *or* 117 Acts 13. 46-49 *or* Acts 26. 19-23 Matthew 25. 31-46 *or* Luke 5. 1-11	Colour of the Season *or* Red	V
21 September	**Matthew, Apostle and Evangelist** *See Lectionary*	**RED**	II
24 September	**Sergei *of* Radonezh (1392), Russian Abbot** **Collect & PC 269 & 383** Jeremiah 17. 7-10 Psalm 119. 57-64 1 John 2. 12-17 Matthew 19. 23-30 *or* Luke 12. 32-34	Colour of the Season *or* White	V
25 September	**Cadoc (6th century), Welsh Abbot** **Collect & PC 152 & 383** Jeremiah 17. 7-10 Psalm 119. 57-64 1 John 2. 12-17 Matthew 19. 23-30 *or* Luke 12. 32-34	White *or* colour of the Season	IV
26 September	**Lancelot Andrewes (1626), Bishop *of* Winchester, Spiritual Writer and Translator of the Scriptures** **Collect & PC 270 & 379** Isaiah 6. 1-8, [9, 10] Psalm 28. 6-9 1 Peter 5. 1-4 *or* Ephesians 4. 7, 8, 11-16 John 21. 15-17	Colour of the Season *or* White	V

Holy Days

Date	Commemoration	Colour	
27 September	**Vincent de Paul (1660), Priest and Beneficent** **Collect & PC 271 & 391** *either* Isaiah 52. 7-10 Psalm 106. 1-4, 19-23 1 Corinthians 1. 25-31 Matthew 25. 34-40 *or* Ezekiel 34. 11-16 Psalm 23 1 Peter 5. 1-4 John 10. 11-16	Colour of the Season *or* White	V
29 September	**Michael *and* All Angels** See Lectionary	**WHITE**	II
30 September	**Jerome (420), Translator of the Scriptures and Doctor of the Faith** **Collect & PC 274 & 392** Sirach 39. 1-9 Psalm 34. 11-18 1 Corinthians 2. 6-13 Matthew 10. 16-23	White *or* colour of the Season	IV
4 October	**Francis *of* Assisi (1226), Friar, Deacon and Peacher** **Collect & PC 275 & 383** *either* Jeremiah 17. 7-10 Psalm 119. 57-64 1 John 2. 12-17 Matthew 19. 23-30 *or* Micah 6. 6-8 Psalm 100 Galatians 6. 14-18 Luke 12. 22-34	White *or* colour of the Season	IV
6 October	**William Tyndale (1536), Translator of the Scriptures and Martyr of the Reformation era** **Collect & PC 276 & 392** Proverbs 8. 4-11 Psalm 46 2 Timothy 3. 12-17 John 3. 14-21 or Luke 9. 57-62	Colour of the Season *or* Red	V
9 October	**Cynog (5th century), Welsh Abbot** **Collect & PC 277 & 383** Jeremiah 17. 7-10 Psalm 119. 57-64 1 John 2. 12-17 Matthew 19. 23-30 *or* Luke 12. 32-34	Colour of the Season *or* White	V

Holy Days

13 October	**Edward the Confessor (1066), King *of* England** **Collect & PC 278 & 389** 2 Samuel 23. 1-5 Psalm 15 1 John 4. 13-16 John 17. 18-23	Colour of the Season *or* White	V
14 October	**Esther John (1960), Missionary and Martyr *in* Pakistan** **Collect & PC 279 & 385** Isaiah 58. 6-11 Psalm 146. 5-10 Romans 8. 35-39 *or* Revelation 7. 13-17 Matthew 10. 24-32 *or* John 15.18 – 16.4a	Colour of the Season *or* Red	V
15 October	**Teresa *of* Avila (1582), Teacher of the faith** **Collect & PC 280 & 356 / 387** Sirach 39. 1-9 Psalm 34. 11-18 Romans 8. 22-27 Matthew 13. 51,52	White *or* colour of the Season	IV
16 October	**Daniel Rowland (1790), Welsh Priest and Preacher** **Collect & PC 281 & 381** *either* Deuteronomy 6. 3-9 Psalm 16 Ephesians 4. 1-7, 11-13 Matthew 25. 14-30 *or* 1 Kings 19. 16, 19-21 Psalm 128 2 Corinthians 5. 14-20 John 15. 9-17	Colour of the Season *or* White	V
17 October	**Ignatius (c117), Bishop of Antioch and Martyr in Rome** **Collect & PC 282 & 385** Wisdom 3. 1-9 Psalm 28. 6-9 Philippians 3. 7-12 John 6. 52-58	Red *or* colour of the Season	IV
18 October	**Luke, Evangelist.** *See Lectionary*	**RED**	II

Holy Days

19 October	**Henry Martyn (1812), Pastor, Translator and Missionary** **Collect & PC 285 & 365 / 392** Isaiah 52. 7-10 Psalm 96. 1-4, 10-13 Acts 13. 46-49 *or* Acts 26 19-23 Mark 16. 15-20	Colour of the Season	V
		or White	
23 October	**James *of* Jerusalem, Bishop and Martyr** **Collect & PC 286 & 377 / 379** Acts 15. 12-22a Psalm 1 1 Corinthians 15. 1-11 Matthew 13. 54-58	Red	IV
		or colour of the Season	
25 October	**Lewis Bayly (1631), Bishop of Bangor and Author** **Collect & PC 287 & 379** Ezekiel 34. 11-16 Psalm 28. 6-9 1 Peter 5. 1-4 *or* Ephesians 4. 7, 8, 11-16 John 21. 15-17	Colour of the Season	V
		or White	
26 October	**Alfred [the Great] (899), King *of* the Anglo-Saxons** **Collect & PC 288 & 389** 2 Samuel 23. 1-5 Psalm 15 Philippians 4. 4-9 John 18. 33-37	Colour of the Season	V
		or White	
28 October	**Simon *and* Jude, Apostles** *See Lectionary*	RED	II
30 October	**Richard Hooker (1600), Priest and Teacher of the faith** **Collect & PC 290 & 356 / 387** Sirach 44. 10-15 Psalm 34. 11-18 1 Corinthians 2. 6-13 John 16. 12-15	Colour of the Season	V
		or White	

Holy Days

Date	Feast / Readings	Colour	Class
31 October	**Catholic and Protestant Saints *and* Martyrs of the Reformation Era** **Collect & PC 291 & 385** Habakkuk 2.1-4 Psalm 46 Romans 1. 16-25 *or* Galatians 2.20 – 3.9 John 3. 14-21 *or* Luke 9. 57-62	Colour of the Season *or* Red	V
	Vigil of All Saints **Collect & PC 292 & 389** Sirach 2. 1-9 Psalm 15 Philippians 4. 4-9 John 17. 18-23	Colour of the Season *or* White	V
1 November	**ALL SAINTS' DAY** *See Lectionary*	**WHITE**	I
2 November	**All Souls' Day** *See Lectionary*	**PURPLE** *or* **BLACK**	II
3 November	**The Saints, Martyrs *and* Confessors *of* our Time** **Collect & PC 294 & 385** Wisdom 3. 1-9 Psalm 28. 6-9 Romans 8. 35-39 *or* Revelation 7. 13-17 Matthew 10. 24-32 *or* John 15.18 – 16.4a	Colour of the Season *or* Red	V
	Winifred (7th century), Welsh Abbess **Collect & PC 295 & 383** Jeremiah 17. 7-10 Psalm 119. 57-64 1 John 2. 12-17 Matthew 19. 23-30 *or* Luke 12. 32-34	Colour of the Season *or* White	V
4 November	**Saints *and* Martyrs of the Anglican Communion** **Collect & PC 296 & 385 / 389** Isaiah 61. 4-9 *or* Sirach 44. 1-15 Psalm 15 Revelation 19. 5-10 John 17. 18-23	Colour of the Season *or* Red	V

Holy Days

5 November	**Cybi (6th century), Welsh Abbot** **Collect & PC 297 & 383** Jeremiah 17. 7-10 Psalm 119. 57-64 1 John 2. 12-17 Matthew 19. 23-30 or Luke 12. 32-34	White *or* colour of the Season	IV
6 November	**Illtud (5th century), Welsh Abbot** **Collect & PC 298 & 383** Jeremiah 17. 7-10 Psalm 119. 57-64 1 John 2. 12-17 Matthew 19. 23-30 or Luke 12. 32-34	White *or* colour of the Season	IV
7 November	**Richard Davies (1581),** **Welsh Bishop and Translator of the Scriptures** **Collect & PC 299 & 392** Malachi 3. 16-18 Psalm 145. 3-13a Revelation 19. 5-8 John 17. 18-23	Colour of the Season *or* White	V
8 November	**The Saints *of* Wales** **Collect & PC 300 & 391** Malachi 3. 16-18 Psalm 145. 3-13a Revelation 19. 5-8 John 17. 18-23	White *or* colour of the Season	IV
10 November	**Leo (461),** **Bishop *of* Rome and Teacher of the Faith** **Collect & PC 301 & 387** Sirach 39. 1-9 Psalm 34. 11-18 1 Peter 5. 1-11 Matthew 13. 51, 52	Colour of the Season *or* White	V
11 November	**Martin (c397), Bishop of Tours** **Collect & PC 302 & 379** Ezekiel 34. 11-16 Psalm 28. 6-9 1 Thessalonians 5. 1-11 Matthew 25. 34-40	White *or* colour of the Season	IV

Holy Days

Date	Commemoration	Colour	
12 November	**Tysilio (6th century), Welsh Abbot** **Collect & PC 303 & 383** Jeremiah 17. 7-10 Psalm 119. 57-64 1 John 2. 12-17 Matthew 19. 23-30 *or* Luke 12. 32-34	Colour of the Season *or* White	V
13 November	**Charles Simeon (1836), Priest and Teacher of the Faith** **Collect & PC 304 & 381** *either* / *or* Malachi 2. 5-7 / Isaiah 52. 7-10 Psalm 23 / Psalm 106. 1-4. 19-23 Colossians 1. 3-8 / 1 Corinthians 4. 1-5 Luke 8. 4-8 / Matthew 23. 8.12	Colour of the Season *or* White	V
14 November	**Dyfrig (6th century), Welsh Bishop** **Collect & PC 305 & 377 / 379** Ezekiel 34. 11-16 Psalm 28. 6-9 1 Peter 5. 1-4 *or* Ephesians 4. 7, 8, 11-16 John 21. 15-17	White *or* colour of the Season	IV
15 November	**The Saints, Martyrs and Missionaries *of* North America** **Collect & PC 306 & 365** Isaiah 52. 7-10 *or* Ezekiel 3. 16-21 Psalm 16 *or* 96. 1-4, 10-13 *or* 117 Acts 13, 46-49 *or* Acts 26, 19-23 Matthew 25. 31-46 *or* Luke 5. 1-11	Colour of the Season *or* Red	V
16 November	**Margaret *of* Scotland (c1045), Queen, Philanthropist and Church Reformer** **Collect & PC 307 & 389** Proverbs 31. 10-12, 20, 26-31 Psalm 15 1 Corinthians 12.13 – 13.3 Matthew 25. 34-46	Colour of the Season *or* White	V

Holy Days

17 November	**Hugh (1200), Bishop *of* Lincoln** **Collect & PC 308 & 377 / 379** Ezekiel 34. 11-16 Psalm 28. 6-9 1 Timothy 6. 11-16 John 21. 15-17	Colour of the Season *or* White	V
18 November	**Hilda (680), Abbess of Whitby** **Collect & PC 309 & 383** Isaiah 61.10 – 62.5 Psalm 119. 57-64 1 John 2. 12-17 Matthew 19. 23-30 *or* Luke 12. 32-34	Colour of the Season *or* White	V
19 November	**Elizabeth *of* Hungary (1231), Princess *of* Thuringia and Philanthropist** **Collect & PC 310 & 389** Proverbs 31. 10-31 Psalm 15 Philippians 4. 4-9 Matthew 25. 31-46	Colour of the Season *or* White	V
21 November	**Paulinus *of* Wales (5th century), Welsh Abbot** **Collect & PC 311 & 383** Jeremiah 17. 7-10 Psalm 119. 57-64 1 John 2. 12-17 Matthew 28. 16-20	Colour of the Season *or* White	V
22 November	**Cecilia (230), Martyr *in* Rome** **Collect & PC 384 & 385** Hosea 2:14-20 Psalm 45:10-17 Matthew 25:1-13	Colour of the Season *or* Red	V
23 November	**Clement (c100), Bishop *of* Rome and Martyr** **Collect & PC 312 & 377 / 379** Ezekiel 34. 11-16 Psalm 28. 6-9 Philippians 3.17 – 4.3 Matthew 16. 13-19	Colour of the Season *or* Red	V

25 November	**John Donne (1631), Priest and Poet** **Collect & PC 313 & 375** Song of Solomon 2. 8-14 Psalm 5. 1-8 Revelation 19. 11-16 John 17. 20-26	Colour of the Season *or* White	V

Rogation and Ember Days

		THE ROGATION DAYS	
Monday, Tuesday and Wednesday before Ascension Day		**Monday** Collect & PC 341 & 344	1 Kings 8. 35-40 Psalm 104. 19-30 1 John 5. 12-15 Matthew 6. 1-15
		Tuesday Collect & PC 342 & 344	Job 28. 1-11 Psalm 107. 1-9 2 Thessalonians 3. 6-13 Mark 11. 22-24
		Wednesday Collect & PC 343 & 344	Deuteronomy 8. 1-10 Psalm 121 Philippians 4. 4-7 Luke 11. 5-13
		EMBER DAYS (Readings used in rotation)	
Wednesday, Friday and Saturday *before*: the third Sunday in advent the second Sunday in Lent *and the nearest Sunday to* 29 June and 29 September		**Set 1** Collect & PC 351 & 352	Jeremiah 1. 4-9 Psalm 84. 8-12 Acts 20. 28-35 Matthew 9. 35-38
		Set 2 Collect & PC 351 & 352	Numbers 11. 16, 17, 24-29 Psalm 122 1 Corinthians 3. 5-11 Luke 4. 16-21 *or* Luke 12. 35-43
		Set 3 Collect & PC 351 & 352	Numbers 27. 15-23 Psalm 134 1 Peter 4. 7-11 John 4. 31-38

Thanksgiving Festivals

	THANKSGIVING FOR HOLY BAPTISM The readings may be used at the Eucharist *or* a non-Eucharistic service		
May be celebrated at any time during Eastertide	Collect & PC 337 & 338 Ezekiel 36. 24-28 Psalm 34. 1-10 Romans 6. 3-11 Matthew 28. 16-20		
	THANKSGIVING FOR THE HARVEST The readings may be used at the Eucharist *or* a non-Eucharistic service		
Traditionally around the first Sunday of October	**Principal Service** Collect & PC 345 & 346		
	YEAR A	YEAR B	YEAR C
	Deuteronomy 8. 7-18 *or* 28. 1-14 Psalm 65 2 Corinthians 9. 6-15 Luke 12. 16-30 *or* 17. 11-19	Joel 2. 21-27 Psalm 126 1 Timothy 2. 1-7 *or* 6. 6-10 Matthew 6. 25-33	Deuteronomy 26. 1-11 Psalm 100 Philippians 4. 4-9 *or* Revelation 14. 14-18 John 6. 25-35
	OT Lessons Deuteronomy 8. 7-20 2 Samuel 24. 18-25 1 Chronicles 29. 10-18 Isaiah 55 Joel 2. 21-27 Sirach 39. 16-27, 32-35 NT Lessons Galatians 5.16 – 6.10 1 John 4. 7-21	Gospels Matthew 13. 24-30 Luke 8. 4-15 John 4. 31-38 John 6. 35-51 Psalm 67 104. 1-23 104. 24-35 145 147 148 150		

155

Dedication Festivals

	DEDICATION FESTIVAL		
Year	Principle Service	Second Service	Third Service
A	Collect & PC 347 & 348 1 Kings 8. 22-30 *or* Revelation 21. 9-14 Psalm 122 Hebrews 12. 18-24 Matthew 21. 12-16	Psalm 132 Jeremiah 7. 1-11 1 Corinthians 3. 9-17	Psalm 48 Haggai 2. 6-9 Hebrews 10. 19-25
B	Collect & PC 347 & 348 Genesis 28. 11-18 or Revelation 21. 9-14 Psalm 122 1 Peter 2. 1-10 John 10. 22-29	Psalm 132 Jeremiah 7. 1-11 Luke 19. 1-10	Psalm 48 Haggai 2. 6-9 Hebrews 10. 19-25
C	Collect & PC 347 & 348 1 Chronicles 29. 6-19 Psalm 122 Ephesians 2. 19-22 John 2. 13-22	Psalm 132 Jeremiah 7. 1-11 Luke 19. 1-10	Psalm 48 Haggai 2. 6-9 Hebrews 10. 19-25

Eucharistic Commons

Abbot / Abbess	1 Kings 19. 9-18 *or* Proverbs 10. 27-32 *or* Song of Solomon 8. 6, 7 *or* Isaiah 61.10 – 62.5 *or* Jeremiah 17. 7-10 *or* Hosea 2. 14, 15, 19, 20
	Psalm 34. 1-8 *or* 112. 1-9 *or* 119. 57-64 *or* 123 *or* 131
	Acts 4. 32-35 *or* 2 Corinthians 10.17 – 11.2 *or* Philippians 3. 7-14 *or* 1 John 2. 12-17 *or* Revelation 19.1, 5-9
	Matthew 11. 25-30 *or* Matthew 19. 3-12 *or* Matthew 19. 23-30 *or* Luke 9. 57-62 *or* Luke 12. 32-3
Bishop	1 Samuel 16.1, 6-13 *or* Isaiah 6. 1-8, [9, 10] *or* Jeremiah 1. 4-10 *or* Ezekiel 3. 16-21 *or* Ezekiel 34. 11-16 *or* Malachi 2. 5-7
	Psalm 1 *or* 15 *or* 16. 5-11 *or* 28. 6-9 *or* 96 *or* 110
	Acts 20. 28-35 *or* 1 Corinthians 4. 1-5 *or* 2 Corinthians 4. 1, 2, [3, 4,] 5-7, [8-10] *or* 2 Corinthians 5. 14-20 *or* Ephesians 4. 7, 8, 11-16 *or* 1 Peter 5. 1-4
	Matthew 11. 25-30 *or* Matthew 24. 42-46 *or* John 10. 11-16 *or* John 15. 9-17 *or* John 21. 15-17
Doctor / Teacher of the Faith	1 Kings 3. [6-10,] 11-14 *or* Proverbs 4. 1-9 *or* Wisdom 7. 7-10, 15, 16 *or* Sirach 39. 1-10
	Psalm 19. 7-10 *or* 34. 11-18 *or* 37. 30-34 *or* 119. 85-96 *or* 119. 97-104
	1 Corinthians 1. 18-25 *or* 1 Corinthians 2. 1-10 *or* 9-16 *or* Ephesians 3. 8-12 *or* 2 Timothy 4. 1-8 *or* Titus 2. 1-8
	Matthew 5. 13-19 *or* 13. 51-58 *or* 23 8-12 *or* Mark 4. 1-9 *or* John 16. 12-15
Martyr	2 Chronicles 24. 17-21 *or* Isaiah 43. 1-7 *or* Jeremiah 11. 18-20 *or* Wisdom 3. 1-9 *or* Wisdom 4. 10-15
	Psalm 3 *or* 11 *or* 28. 6-9 *or* 31. 1-5 *or* 44. 13-21 *or* 126
	Romans 8. 35-39 *or* 2 Corinthians 4. 7-15 *or* 2 Timothy 2. 3-7, [8-13] *or* Hebrews 11. 32-40 *or* 1 Peter 4. 12-19 *or* Revelation 7. 13-17 *or* Revelation 12. 10-12a
	Matthew 10. 16-22 *or* Matthew 10. 24-39 *or* Matthew 16. 24-26 *or* John 12. 24-26 *or* John 15.18 – 16.4a
Mission	Isaiah 49. 1-6 *or* Isaiah 52. 7-10 *or* Micah 4. 1-5
	Psalm 2 *or* 46 *or* 67 *or* 96. 1-4, 10-13
	Acts 17. 12-34 *or* 2 Corinthians 5.14 – 6.2 *or* Ephesians 2. 13-22
	Matthew 5. 13-16 *or* Matthew 9. 35-38 *or* Matthew 28.16-20 *or* John 17. 20-26

Eucharistic Commons

Missionary	Isaiah 52. 7-10 *or* Isaiah 61. 1-3a *or* Ezekiel 3. 16-21 *or* Ezekiel 34. 11-16 *or* Jonah 3. 1-5
	Psalm 16 *or* 67 *or* 87 *or* 96. 1-4, 10-13 *or* 97 *or* 100 *or* 117
	Acts 2. 14, 22-36 *or* Acts 13. 46-49 *or* Acts 16. 6-10 *or* Acts 26. 19-23 *or* Romans 15. 17-21 *or* 2 Corinthians 5.11 – 6.2
	Matthew 9. 35-38 *or* Matthew 25. 31-46 *or* Matthew 28. 16-20 *or* Mark 16. 15-20 *or* Luke 5. 1-11 *or* Luke 10. 1-9
Pastor	*either* *or* Isaiah 52. 7-10 Ezekiel 34. 11-16 Psalm 106. 1-4, 19-23 Psalm 23 1 Corinthians 4. 1-5 1 Peter 5. 1-4 Matthew 23. 8-12 John 10. 11-16
Poet or Artist	Song of Solomon 2. 8-14 Psalm 5. 1-8 Revelation 19. 11-16 John 17. 20-26
Priest	*either* *or* Deuteronomy 6. 3-9 1 Kings 19. 16, 19-21 Psalm 16 Psalm 128 Ephesians 4. 1-7, 11-13 2 Corinthians 5. 14-20 Matthew 25. 14-30 John 15. 9-17
Any Saint	Genesis 12. 1-4 *or* Proverbs 8, 1-11 *or* Micah 6. 6-8 *or* Sirach 2. 1-9, [10-17]
	Psalm 15 *or* 32 *or* 33. 1-5 *or* 119. 1-8 *or* 139. 1-6, [7-12] *or* 145. 8-13
	Ephesians 3. 14-19 *or* 6. 11-18 *or* Philippians 4. 4-9 *or* Hebrews 13. 7, 8, 15, 16 *or* James 2. 14-17 *or* 1 John 4. 7-16 *or* Revelation 21. [1-4,] 5-7
	Matthew 19. 16-21 *or* Matthew 25. 1-13 *or* Matthew 25. 14-30 *or* John 15. 1-8 *or* John 17. 18-26
Saint of Wales	Malachi 3. 16-18 Psalm 145. 3-13a Revelation 19. 5-8 John 17. 18-23

Eucharistic Commons

Social Responsibility / A Social Reformer	Isaiah 32. 15-20 *or* Amos 5. 21-24 *or* Amos 8. 4-7 *or* Sirach 4. 1-10
	Psalm 31. 21-24 *or* 72. 1-4, 12-14 *or* 85. 1-7 *or* 146. 5-10
	Acts 5. 1-11 *or* Colossians 3. 12-15 *or* James 2. 1-4
	Matthew 5. 1-12 *or* Matthew 25. 31-46 *or* Mark 2. 1-5 *or* Luke 16. 19-31
Civic Occasions	Joshua 1. 1-9 *or* Proverbs 8. 1-16 *or* Isaiah 26. 1-8
	Psalm 20 *or* 47 *or* 101 *or* 121
	Romans 13. 1-10 *or* Revelation 21.22 – 22.4
	Matthew 22. 16-22 *or* Mark 12. 13-17 *or* Luke 22. 24-30
Education	Deuteronomy 6. 4-9, 20-25 *or* Proverbs 8. 22-31 *or* Sirach 44. 1-15
	Psalm 36. 5-10 *or* 49. 1-4 *or* 78. 1-7
	Philippians 4. 7, 8 *or* 2 Timothy 3.14 – 4.5
	Matthew 11. 25-30 *or* Matthew 13. 44-46 *or* John 7. 14-18
Reformation	Habakkuk 2. 1-4
	Psalm 46
	Romans 1. 16-25 *or* Galatians 2.20 – 3.9
	John 3. 14-21 *or* Luke 9. 57-62
Vigil of Saints	Exodus 19. 3-6a
	Psalm 92. 1, 2, 12, 13
	Revelation 5. 6-10
	Luke 6. 20-23
Unity	*Dated ecumenical material may be used*
	Jeremiah 33. 6-9a *or* Ezekiel 36. 23-28 *or* Ezekiel 37. 15-22 *or* Zephaniah 3. 16-20
	Psalm 100 *or* 122 *or* 133
	Ephesians 4. 1-6 *or* Colossians 3. 9-17 *or* 1 John 4. 9-15
	Matthew 18. 19-22 *or* John 11. 45-52 *or* John 17. 11b-23
Any Need	Genesis 9. 8-17 *or* Job 1. 13-22 *or* Isaiah 38. 6-11 *or* Isaiah 40. 28-31
	Psalm 86. 1-7 *or* 107. 4-16 *or* 121 *or* 142
	Romans 3. 21-26 *or* Romans 8. 18-25 *or* 2 Corinthians 8. 1-5, 9
	Mark 4. 35-41 *or* Mark 11. 22-25 *or* Luke 12. 1-7 *or* John 16. 31-33

Peace	Isaiah 9. 1-6 *or* Isaiah 57. 15-19 *or* Micah 4. 1-5
	Psalm 29. 1-4, 10, 11 *or* 40.13-17 *or* 72. 1-7 *or* 85. 8-13
	Philippians 4. 6-9 *or* 1 Timothy 2. 1-6 *or* James 3. 13-18
	Matthew 5. 43-48 *or* John 14. 23-29 *or* John 15. 9-17
The Guidance of the Holy Spirit / A Meeting	Proverbs 24. 3-7 *or* Isaiah 30. 15-21 *or* Isaiah 61. 1-3 *or* Wisdom 9. 13-17
	Psalm 25. 1-9 *or* 86. 9-12, 16, 17 *or* 104. 24-34 *or* 143. 8-10
	Acts 15. 23-29 *or* Romans 8. 22-27 *or* 1 Corinthians 12. 4-13
	John 14. [15-22,] 23-26 *or* John 14. 27-33 *or* John 16. 13-15
Marriage / Sickness / The Dying *or* Funerals	See orders of service

Notes

Notes